in his own words

bob dylan

Christian Williams

OMNIBUS PRESS
LONDON · NEW YORK · PARIS · SYDNEY

Copyright © 1993 Omnibus Press
(A Division of Book Sales Limited)

Edited by Chris Charlesworth.
Cover & book designed by Michael Bell Design.
Picture research by David Brolan.

ISBN 0.7119.3213.1
Order No OP 47157.

Exclusive distributors:
Book Sales Limited
8/9 Frith Street,
London W1V 5TZ, UK.

Music Sales Corporation,
257 Park Avenue South,
New York, NY 10010, USA.

Music Sales Pty Limited
120 Rothschild Avenue,
Rosebery, NSW 2018, Australia.

To the Music Trade only:
Music Sales Limited
8/9 Frith Street,
London W1V 5TZ, UK.

Picture credits: front cover: London Features International
Jack Barron/SIN: 74t; Fin Costello/Redferns: 111; Harry Goodwin: 12t&b, 20; Bob Gruen/Star File:
30, 35, 42, 48, 50, 66, 67, 69, 70, 75, 91, 94, 96, 109; Mike Guastella/Star File: 106; Elliott Landy/
Redferns: 15; LFI: 4, 6, 7, 8, 10, 11t, 21, 22, 23, 31, 33, 34, 36, 41, 49, 52, 53b, 55, 58, 62/63, 71, 72,
73, 74b, 77, 80, 81t, 83b, 84, 86, 89, 92, 93, 95, 97, 98, 100, 102, 103, 104, 108t, 110; Jeffrey Mayer/
Star File: 99; Barry Plummer: 43, 46, 54, 108b; Pictorial Press: 9, 14, 16, 19, 24, 26, 28, 40, 107;
Chuck Pulin/Star File: 45, 53t, 78t, 101, 105; Relay Photos: 25, 61, 64, 78b, 112; Brian Shuel/
Redferns: 11b, 18, 39, 79; Joe Sia/Star File: 47; Warner Bros: 56, 57; Val Wilmer/Redferns: 38;
Vinnie Zuffante/Star File: 60, 81b, 83t.

A catalogue record for this book is available from the British Library.

Printed in Great Britain by Page Bros, Norwich.

introduction

Bob Dylan doesn't mince words. Neither does he suffer fools gladly.
Yet no entertainer's words have been studied, analysed, interpreted and
discussed as those of the song and dance man whose influence on rock
has been as profound as any in the second half of the twentieth century.

He has been called the spokesman for his generation and for
millions of people his music can evoke the experience of growing up
in the Sixties. The songs he wrote in the Sixties paralleled the general
direction of the youth movement: beginning with the Greenwich
Village folk revival through protest against the Vietnam war and other
obscenities, experiments with drugs, the charms of rural life, religious
conversion and subsequent disillusionment.

Though he has been making records since 1961 he has given
surprisingly few interviews. In the first flowering of his career he faced
several press conferences but his answers were often glib responses to
dull, uncomprehending journalists from the straight media whose grasp
of Dylan's character and work was minimal. After his motor bike crash
in 1966 he remained incommunicable for 18 months and between
1969 and 1975 he gave only one major interview. Alternately there
have been periods when Dylan talked a great deal, particularly in
more recent years on occasions when his acerbic character appeared
at times to mellow with age. Consequently there are some periods
of his career where we know his opinions in great detail and
others where we know little.

Even when Dylan did give interviews we are faced with problems.
As a struggling folk singer anxious to make a name for himself, he often
fabricated stories about his early life. This is nothing new for imaginative
rock stars, but Dylan was certainly amongst the first to romanticise
his past in order to create a myth which he found more acceptable
than a mundane truth. Later he reacted to stupidity on the part of
newsmen by replying to their questions with strings of surrealistic and
often very humorous images. Many of these make little sense when
taken out of context.

The quotes collected here have been taken from newspapers and
magazine interviews and transcribed from rare tapes of TV and radio
interviews and talk shows. They take in 30 years and provide a valuable
insight into the attitudes, ideas, wit and humour that make up Dylan
the man as well as Dylan the songwriter and performer.

early life

I was never going to be anything else, never. I was playing when I was twelve years old, and all I wanted to do was play my guitar. (New York, 1985)

I always wanted to be a guitar player and singer. Since I was ten, eleven or twelve it was all that interested me. That was the only thing that I did that meant anything really. 'Henrietta' was the first rock'n'roll record I heard. Before that I'd listen to Hank Williams a lot. Before that, Johnny Ray. He was the first singer whose voice and style, I guess, I totally fell in love with. There was just something about the way he sang 'When Your Sweetheart Sends A Letter'... that just knocked me out. I loved his style, wanted to dress like him too, that was really early though. I ran into him in the elevator in Sydney, Australia, late in '78 and told him he impressed me so when I was growing up... I still have a few of his records. (New York, 1985)

You know, where I'm from I only heard Country music from Hank Williams, Hank Snow, Hank Payne. (New York, 1980)

I started singing... when I was about ten - ten or eleven - and started out just country and western - Hank Williams, Lefty Frizzell kind of things. (Los Angeles, 1966)

The town didn't have a rabbi, and it was time for me to be bar-mitzvahed. Suddenly a rabbi showed up under strange circumstances for only a year. He and his wife got off the bus in the middle of winter. He showed up just in time for me to learn this stuff. He was an old man from Brooklyn who had a white beard and wore a black hat and black clothes. They put him upstairs above the café, which was the local hangout. It was a rock'n'roll café where I used to hang out, too. I used to go there every day to learn this stuff, either after school or after dinner. After studying with him for an hour or so, I'd come down and boogie. (New York, 1985)

I left where I'm from because there's nothing there... when I left there, I knew one thing. I had to get out of there and not come back. Just from my senses I knew there was something more than Walt Disney movies. (New York, 1965)

I'm not the only one that left there and travelled around... everybody left there. I don't know really of anybody that stayed there. (New York, 1965)

Minneapolis was the first big city I lived in if you want to call
it that. I came out of the wilderness and just naturally fell in with
the beat scene, the bohemian, Be Bop crowd, it was all pretty
much connected... it was Jack Kerouac, Ginsberg, Corso,
Ferlinghetti... I got in at the tail end of that and it was magic.
(New York, 1978)

I'd fell in with a new kind a people there in Minneapolis.
I was going to new kids a parties an' thinkin' new kinds a things...
I read into what I was doing an' saw myself romantically breakin'
off all ties with all things of the established order, although
I'd never really been accepted by that order anyway... what I saw
connected with the fraternity house summed up the whole
established world. (New York, 1963)

By that time I was singing stuff like 'Ruby Lee' by The Sunny
Mountain Boys, and 'Jack O'Diamonds' by Odetta and somehow
because of my earlier rock'n'roll background was unconsciously
crossing the two styles. This made me different from your regular
folk singers, who were either folk song purists or concert-hall

singers, who just happened to be singing folk songs. I'd played by myself with just a guitar and harmonica or as a duo with Spider Jack Koerner, who played mostly ballads and Josh White type blues. He knew more songs than I did. 'Whoa Boys Can't Ya Line', 'M, John Hardy', 'Golden Vanity', I learned all those from him. We sounded great, not unlike The Delmore Brothers. I could always hear my voice sounding better as a harmony singer. In New York, I worked off and on with Mark Spoelstra and later with Jim Kweskin. Jim and I sounded pretty similar to Cisco and Woody! (New York, 1985)

The first thing that turned me on to folk singing was Odetta. I heard a record of hers in a record store, back when you could listen to records there in the store. That was in '58 or something like that. Right then and there, I went out and traded my electric guitar and amplifier for an acoustical guitar, a flat-top Gibson... Anyway, from Odetta, I went to Harry Belafonte, The Kingston Trio, little by little uncovering more as I went along. Finally, I was doing nothing but Carter Family and Jesse Fuller songs. (Malibu, 1978)

I'd learned as much as I could and used up all my options... When I arrived in Minneapolis it had seemed like a big city or a big town. When I left it was like some rural outpost. (New York, 1985)

Family

When I was young my life was built around the family. We got together all the time. There weren't many Jews around. (Malibu, 1978)

My grandfather had come over from Russia in the 1920s. He was a peddler and made shoes... My father was a very active man, but he was stricken very early by an attack of polio. The illness put an end to all his dreams... when we moved from the North of the country, two of his brothers, who were electrical fitters, opened a shop and they took him with them so that he could mind the shop. (Malibu, 1978)

My family settled in Hibbing I think in about '46 or '47. My father had polio when I was very young. There was a big epidemic. He lost his job in Duluth and we moved to the Iron range and moved in with my grandmother Florence and grandfather who was still alive at the time. (New York, 1978)

Talkin' New York

I knew I had to get to New York... I'd been dreaming
about that for a long time.
(New York, 1985)

I just got up one morning and left. I'd spent so much time
thinking about it I couldn't think about it any more. Snow or
no snow, it was time for me to go. I made a lot of friends and
I guess some enemies too, but I had used up all my options.
It all got real old real fast. I stood on the highway during a
blizzard snowstorm believing in the mercy of the world and
headed East, didn't have nothing but my guitar and suitcase.
That was my whole world. The first ride I got, you know,
was from some old guy in a jalopy, sort of a Bela Lugosi type,
who carried me into Wisconsin. Of all the rides I've ever
gotten it's the only one that stands out in my mind.
People hitch-hiked a lot back then. It was real natural.
I wouldn't do that today. People aren't as friendly and there's
too many drugs on the road.
(New York, 1985)

New York was a dream ... It was a dream of cosmopolitan
riches of the mind. It was the greatest place for me to learn
and to meet other people who were on similar journeys...
Back then there were no pressures... you know, I mean, music
people were like a bunch of cotton pickers. They see you on the
side of the road, but nobody stops to give a shit. I mean, it wasn't
that important. So Washington Square was a place where people
you knew or met congregated every Sunday and it was like a
world of music... There could be fifteen jug bands, five bluegrass
bands and an old crummy string band, twenty Irish confederate
groups, a Southern mountain band, folk singers of all kinds and
colours singing John Henry work songs... Bongo drums, conga
drums, saxophone players, drummers of all nations and
nationalities. Poets who would rant and rave from the statues.
You know, those things don't happen any more. But then
that was what was happening. It was all street. Cafés would
be open all night. It was a European thing that never really
took off. It has never really been a part of this country.
That is what New York was like when I got there... Mass
communication killed it. It turned it into one big carnival
sideshow. That was what I sensed, and I got out of there when
it was starting to happen. The atmosphere changed from one
of creativity and isolation to one where the attention would be
turned more to the show.
(Los Angeles, 1978)

There was a luncheonette place where we used to go all the time, and just sort of hung around... a bunch of singers used to go in there. You could stay there all day, and it was open all night. Back there, you lived in restaurants a lot. Now they don't quite feel that homey. (New York, 1985)

Where I come from there was always plenty of snow so I was used to that, but going to New York was like going to the Moon. You just didn't get on a plane and go there, you know. New York! Ed Sullivan, the New York Yankees, Broadway, Harlem... you might as well have been talking about China. It was some place which not too many people went to, and anybody who did go never came back. (New York, 1978)

The worst time of my life came when I tried to find something in the past. Like when I went back to New York for the second time. I didn't know what to do. Everything had changed.
(Los Angeles, 1989)

Woody Guthrie.

Idols & heroes

All the music I heard up until I left Minnesota was... I didn't hear any folk music... I just heard Country and Western, rock and roll and polka music.

Who were the ones you especially dug? Country and Western let's say?

Just about all the people... Lefty Frizell...all those people like that.

And rock and roll?

All the people that were around. Elvis Presley, Carl Perkins, Gene Vincent, Buddy Holly, Jerry Lee Lewis.

And then what was added on like in the folk field?

Well, then it came down to the fact that to make it alone you had to play alone, y'know. I discovered folk music where people actually played alone. First it started with Odetta... no, it starts with Harry Belafonte and then right away you know he's not really where it's at.

Why ?

Well, you know right away you haven't got that much time to sit down and Harry Belafonte doesn't know that many songs. And then Odetta, and you go through these stages until finally you arrive at Woody Guthrie who sounds pretty weird and obviously looks like you to some degree and I went through all Woody Guthrie's songs and then the folk music which I'd heard to some degree...and I listened to all that music.

After Guthrie, was there anybody in particular?

No, not really. Woody Guthrie hasn't influenced what I'm doing now. He hasn't had too much to do with these past two records. In fact, he hasn't really had any influence at all on these past two records. The influence has all been on the first record, second record, third record, on the fourth it was kind of wearing off a little bit. When I say influence, I mean total influence. I mean either writing or singing, y'know. I mean his influence in his manner of speaking. His influence in his topics that he writes about. His influence lies in his phrasing and stuff like that. (New York, 1965)

The most inspiring type of entertainer for me has always been somebody like Jimmie Rodgers, somebody who could do it alone and was totally original. He was combining elements of blues and hill billy sounds before anyone else had thought of it. He recorded at the same time as Blind Willie McTell but he wasn't just another white boy singing black. That was his great genius and he was there first... he sang in a plaintive voice and style and he's outlasted them all. (New York, 1985)

I was lucky to meet Lonnie Johnson at the same club I was working and I must say he greatly influenced me. You can hear it in that first record, I mean 'Corina, Corina'... that's pretty much Lonnie Johnson. I used to watch him and sometimes he'd let me play with him. (New York, 1978)

I was pretty fanatical about what I wanted to do, so after learning about two hundred of Woody's songs, I went to see him and I waited for the right moment to visit him in a hospital in Morristown, New Jersey. I took a bus from New York, sat with him and sang his songs. (New York, 1984)

My biggest idol on stage I think, even off stage, running all through my head all the time was Charlie Chaplin. (New York, 1962)

I think of a hero as someone who understands the degree of responsibility that comes with his freedom, someone who's not afraid to jump in front of a freight train to save a loved one's life, to draw a crowd with my guitar, that's about the most heroic thing that I can do. To play a song to calm a king, well, everybody don't get to do that. (New York, 1985)

Who do you admire?

Who is there to admire now? Some world leader? Who?
I could probably think of many people actually that I admire.
There's a guy who works in a gas station in LA - an old guy
I truly admire that guy.

What's he done?

What's he done? He helped me fix my carburettor once.
(Toronto, 1986)

Changes name to Bob Dylan

I didn't create Bob Dylan, Bob Dylan has always been here...
always was. When I was a child, there was Bob Dylan... sometimes
your parents don't even know who you are.
(Los Angeles, 1978)

I needed a name in a hurry and I picked that one. It just
came to me as I was standing there ... Wasn't Dylan Thomas at
all, it just came to me. I knew about Dylan Thomas of course,
but I didn't deliberately pick his name. (New York, 1968)

I've done more for Dylan Thomas than he's ever done for me.
(New York, 1966)

song & dance man

Folk music

Folk Music was very split up, there was a purist side to it.
You know, many people didn't want to hear it if you couldn't
play the song exactly the way that Aunt Molly Jackson played it.
I just kind of blazed my way through all that kind of stuff.
(Los Angeles, 1984)

There were a bunch of people who helped me out in the
very early Sixties. Ewan MacColl and Peggy Seeger had a club
and one night Martin Carthy brought me down there to play.
At that time there was all those ballads and the only place you
could get them was like Southern Mountain kinda ballads
but they'd been one step removed from the real old time
ballads that were from the old country. There were a bunch
of people that helped me out in the very early Sixties Martin
Carthy, Bob Davenport... just a lot of folk singer type people
who ran into me. It was before ... well The Marquee Club
was happening then. Who was playing there then? Alex?
Alex Korner. Alexis Korner. That was happening. Blues.
A lot of my early stuff was taken from all the stuff that
those guys taught me then.

Are you one of the great white Blues singers?

Probably not... if that's a category. Who wants to be called
that? Jimmie Rodgers was that, if anything. People call him
a white blues singer.

Do you still feel most at home with the blues?

Well only because the structure is so simple and you can
say what you want to say in such an immediate kinda way.
Just two lines and the one line. And the form is rather
attractive because it's so simple. (New York, 1989)

There was a clique, you know. Folk Music was a strict and
rigid establishment. If you sang Southern Mountain Blues,
you didn't sing Southern Mountain Ballads and you didn't sing
City Blues. If you sang Texas Cowboy songs, you didn't play
English Ballads. It was really pathetic. (New York, 1985)

Who do you think is the best folk singer in the world?

Oh, Peter Lorre.
(London, 1966)

Dylan performs at The Singles Club in London during his first visit to the UK in 1963.

I wonder if you could tell me, among folk singers, how many could be classified as protest singers today?

I don't understand. Could you ask the question again?

How many people who labour in the same musical vineyards in which you toil, how many are protest singers? That is, how many use their music to protest about the social state in which we are today?

How many? One hundred thirty-six.
(Los Angeles, 1965)

Folk singing is just a bunch of fat people.
(San Francisco, 1965)

People don't know folk songs any more. I mean, hardly anybody sings them any more, and people think that people who play the acoustic guitar and write their own songs are folk singers, but that's not necessarily true. They're writing their own songs, but they're not really based on anything. So I thought, well, if I'm going around again, I'm going to sing folk songs, because first of all, I love them and the lyrics in them are - I mean they're incredible stories, and that's where I got a lot of my stuff from in the early years - and still do. Folk songs are still better - even though they're not commercial - they're still better than ninety percent of the stuff you hear on the radio. (New York, 1985)

Protest songs

Sure you can make all sorts of protest songs and put them out
on a Folkways record. But who hears them?
(Santa Monica, 1965)

Are you a protest singer?

No, I sing mathematical songs... I deal with subjects like hunger
Angeles, 1965)

in your songs. Does that mean you're protesting
t you're angry about?

m a delightful sort of person.

ing protest songs?

said that?

that. I said so you don't sing protest songs any more.

protest.

With Joan Baez in London, 1965.

Folk rock

It's not folk rock, it's just instruments.
(Los Angeles, 1965)

It's easy for people to classify it as rock & roll, to put
it down. Rock & roll is a straight twelve-bar blues progression.
My new songs aren't. I used to play rock & roll a long time ago,
before I even started playing old-fashioned folk.
(Santa Monica, 1965)

I was doing fine, you know, singing and playing my
guitar. It was a sure thing... I was getting very bored with that.
I couldn't go out and play like that. I was thinking of quitting.
Out front it was a sure thing. I know what the audience was
going to do, how they would react. It was very automatic... What
I'm doing now, it's a whole other thing. We're not playing rock
music. It's not a hard sound. These people call it folk-rock -
if they want to call it that, something that simple, it's good for
selling records. As far as it being what it is, I don't know what
it is. I can't call it folk-rock. It's a whole way of doing things.
(Los Angeles, 1965)

the real message

Do you have any important philosophy for the world?

I don't drink hard liquor, if that's what you mean.

No, the world in general. You and the world?
Are you kidding? The world don't need me. Christ, I'm only five feet ten. (Los Angeles, 1965)

What are your songs all about?

It's beyond me, man. I just go out there and sing them.
If people are y'know... wherever I'm booked to play I just go out there and sing them and I don't try to get anybody to listen. (Manchester, 1965)

What is your real message?

My real message? Keep a good head and always carry a light bulb. (London, 1965)

Folk hero turns electric

There were a lot of people there [at Newport] who were very pleased that I got booed. I saw them afterward. I do resent somewhat, though, that everybody that booed said they did it because they were old fans. (Los Angeles, 1966)

I did this very crazy thing. I didn't know what was going to happen, but they certainly booed, I'll tell you that. You could hear it all over the place. (San Francisco, 1965)

I had a hit record out so I don't know how people expected me to do anything different. (Los Angeles, 1985)

The motorcycle accident

The back wheel locked, I think. I lost control, swerving from left to right. Next thing I know I was someplace I'd never heard of - Middletown, I think - with my face cut up so I got some scars and my neck busted up pretty good. I saw my whole life pass in front of me. (1966)

I didn't sense the importance of that accident until at
least a year after that. I realised [then] that it was a real accident.
I mean I thought that I was just gonna get up and go back to
doing what I was doing before... but I couldn't do it any
more. (Woodstock, 1969)

The turning point was back in Woodstock. A little after the
accident. Sitting around one night under a full moon, I looked
out into the bleak woods and I said, 'Something's gotta change.'
There was some business that had to be taken care of.
(New York, 1974)

What was I doing? I don't know. It came time. Was it when
I had the motorcycle accident? Well, I was straining pretty hard
and couldn't have gone on living that way much longer.
The fact that I had made it through what I did is pretty
miraculous. But, you know, sometimes you get too close to
something and you got to get away from it to be able to
see it. And something like that happened to me at the time.
Those were in my wild unnatural moments. I'm glad those
feelings passed. (Malibu, 1978)

What I survived after that was even harder to survive than the
motorcycle crash. That was just a physical crash, but sometimes
there are things in life that you cannot see, that are harder to
survive than something which you can pin down.
(Los Angeles, 1978)

[When] I had that motorcycle accident... I woke up
and caught my senses, I realised I was just workin' for all
these leeches. And I didn't want to do that. Plus, I had a
family, and I just wanted to see my kids.
(New York, 1984)

It was real early in the morning on top of a hill near
Woodstock. I can't even remember how it happened. I was
blinded by the sun... I was drivin' right straight into the sun,
and I looked up into it even though I remember someone
telling me a long time ago when I was a kid never to look
straight at the sun... I went blind for a second and I kind of
panicked or something. I stomped down on the brake and
the rear wheel locked up on me and I went flyin'... [Sara]
was followin' me in a car. She picked me up. Spent a week
in the hospital, then they moved me to this doctor's house
in town. In his attic. Had a bed up there in his attic with
a window lookin' out. Sara stayed there with me.
(New York, 1987)

writing & performing

Does the focus on your initial work suggest that you have already painted your masterpiece?

An easy way out would be to say, 'Yeah, it's all behind me, that's it and there's no more.' But you want to say there might be a small chance that something up there will surpass whatever you did. Everybody works in the shadow of what they've previously done. But you have to overcome that ...
(*USA Today*, 1989)

Poetry

You don't necessarily have to write to be a poet. Some people work in gas stations and they're poets. I don't call myself a poet because I don't like the word. I'm a trapeze artist.
(Los Angeles, 1965)

I didn't start writing poetry until I was out of high school. I was eighteen or so when I discovered Ginsberg, Gary Snyder, Philip Whalen, Frank O'Hara and those guys. Then I went back and started reading French guys, Rimbaud and François Villon. (New York, 1985)

Writing

One time I wanted to write a novel; and so I was putting a lot of time in. It must have been about six months off and on... and finally I just came to the conclusion... Is this gonna be THE novel, THE statement? Is this my message? My Thing? And no matter how many pages - I had about five hundred pages of it - I said, 'No, of course not.' That's bullshit. This is nothing. If I finish this novel, it's not gonna come out until at least a year and a half to two years from now. It's gonna be a completely different thing by the time it does come out ... Meantime, I'm not even gonna be there any more. It won't be me that wrote the novel. And from then on I have to live up to that novel... People are gonna ask me what I'm doing... I'm gonna HAVE to say I'M writing another novel!
(Los Angeles, 1965)

All my writing goes into songs now. Other forms don't interest me any more. (Los Angeles, 1966)

I wrote wherever I happened to be. Sometimes I'd spend a whole day sitting at a corner table in a coffee-house just writing whatever came into my head ... just anything. I'd look at people for hours and I'd make up things about them, or I'd think what kind of song would they like to hear and I'd make one up. (New York, 1965)

I don't think when I write. I just react and put it down on paper. I'm serious about everything I write. For instance, I get mad when I see friends of mine sitting in Southern jails, getting their heads beat in. What comes out of the music is a call to action. (New York, 1963)

Songs

People can learn everything about me through my songs, if they know where to look. They can juxtapose them with certain other songs and draw a clear picture. (New York, 1990)

When I'm singing my songs, it never occurs to me that I wrote them. If I didn't have a song like 'Masters Of War', I'd find a song like 'Masters Of War' to sing. Same thing with 'Times They Are A-Changin'. (Hamilton, Ontario, 1988)

None of my songs are what you call 'top singles'. Singles get dated. You hear a lot of groups, there's a lot of groups going around and they fall into an Oldies type bag, right? A nostalgia trip. Well, that's because these people have had hit singles. (New York, 1989)

For me none of the songs I've written has really dated. They capture something I've never been able to improve on, whatever their statement is ... People say they're 'nostalgia', but I don't know what that means really. 'A Tale Of Two Cities' was written one hundred years ago - is that nostalgic? This term 'nostalgic', it's just another way people have of dealing with you and putting you some place they think they understand. It's just another label. (Hamburg, 1984)

If I liked a song, I would just learn it and sing it the only way I could play it. (New York, 1985)

The words of the songs aren't written out just for the paper, they're written so you can read [them] ... If you take away whatever there is to the song - the beat, the melody - I could still recite it ... It ain't the melodies that're important, man, it's the words. I don't give a damn about the melodies. (New York, 1963)

I used to think that myself and my songs were the same thing. But I don't believe that any more. There's myself and there's my song, which I hope is everybody's song. (Woodstock, 1968)

When I started writing ... there wasn't anybody else doing things like that. Woody Guthrie had done similar things but he hadn't really done that type of song. Besides, I had learned from Woody Guthrie and knew and could sing anything he had done. But now the time had changed and things would be different. He contributed a lot to my style lyrically and dynamically but my musical background had been different, with rock 'n' roll and rhythm and blues playing a big part earlier on. Actually, attitude had more to do with it than technical ability and that's what the folk movement lacked. In other words, I played all the folk songs with a rock 'n' roll attitude. This is what made me different and allowed me to cut through all the mess and be heard. (New York, 1985)

I didn't know at the time but all the radio songs were written at Tin Pan Alley, the Brill Building. They had stables of song writers up there that provided songs for artists. I heard of it but didn't pay much attention. They were good songwriters

but the world they knew and the world I knew were totally
different. Most of the songs, though, being recorded came
from there, I guess because most singers didn't write their
own. They didn't think about it. Anyway, Tin Pan Alley is gone.
I put an end to it. People can record their own songs now.
They're almost expected to do it. The funny thing about
it though is that I didn't start out as a songwriter. I just
drifted into it. Those other people had it down to a science.
(New York, 1985)

Songwriting

You never know what you're going to write. You never even know if you're going to make another record, really.
(New York, 1985)

I just wanted a song to sing, and there came a certain point where I couldn't sing anything. So I had to write what I wanted to sing 'cause nobody else was writing what I wanted to sing. I couldn't find it anywhere. If I could I probably would never have started writing. (New York, 1984)

I began writing because I was singing. That's the important thing. I started writing because things were changing all the time and a certain song needed to be written. I started writing them because I wanted to sing them. Anyway, one thing led to another and I just kept on writing my own songs, but I stumbled into it really. It was nothing I had prepared myself for, but I did sing a lot of songs before I wrote any of my own. I think that's important too. (New York, 1985)

I used to write songs, like I'd say, 'Yeah, what's bad, pick out something bad, like segregation, OK here we go,' and I'd pick one of the thousand million little points I can pick and explode it, some of them which I didn't know about. I wrote a song about

'Emmett Till', which in all honesty was a bullshit song... I realise
now that my reasons and motives behind it were phoney.
I didn't have to write it. (New York, 1964)

It's hard to be free in a song - getting it all in. Songs are so
confining. Woody Guthrie told me once that songs don't have to
do anything like that. But it's not true. A song has to have some
kind of form to fit the music. You can bend the metre, but it still
has to fit somehow. I've been getting freer in the songs I write,
but I still feel confined. That's why I write a lot of poetry, if
that's the word. Poetry can make its own form.
(New York, 1964)

I make a song as small or as narrow as possible rather
than make it a big, broad, grand thing. By keeping it so narrow,
emotion plays a great part. (New York, 1987)

What I do is write songs and sing them and perform them.
Anything else trying to get on top of it, making something out
of it which it isn't just brings me down.
(San Francisco, 1965)

I have to make a new song out of what I know and out of
what I'm feeling. (New York, 1974)

I'll do anything to write a song ... I used to anyway.
(Malibu, 1978)

There's no rule that claims that anyone must write their
own songs. And I do. I write a lot of songs. But so what, you
know. You could take another song somebody else has written
and make it yours ... Every so often you've gotta sing songs
that're out there ... Writing is such an isolated thing. You're in
such an isolated frame of mind. You have to get into or be
in that place. In the old days, I could get to it real quick.
I can't get to it like that no more. (Los Angeles, 1988)

There's a version [of 'Tangled Up In Blue'] we used to do
on stage with just electric guitar and saxophone - keeping the
same lyrics, thinking that maybe if I did that to it it would
bring it out in an emotional way. So I changed the lyrics to
bring it up to date. But I didn't change it 'cause I was singing
it one night and thought, 'Oh, I'm bored with the old words.'
The old ones were never quite filled in. I re-wrote it in a
hotel room somewhere. I think it was in Amsterdam ...
When I sang it the next night I knew it was right.
(Rotterdam, 1985)

With Tom Petty.

*Does anyone intervene where the lyrics are concerned or is it
solely your area?*

No one has ever said to me, change that lyric. Make it more
this way or that way. I mean, that might be an unfortunate thing
that no one has ever done that... Sometimes you wish
somebody would. (New York, 1989)

*Is it easier to write when you're miserable? Is writing when you're
happy more difficult than when you're unhappy?*

Well, you try to do neither actually. You really don't want
to... as strange as it might sound... it's just as easy to write from
a miserable point of view on something where you're projecting
a great deal of contentment and in the same way it's easy to write
from a great deal of contentment about something that you're
projecting a lot of misery into. The way you do it, that's a
different thing. What style you use. What vocabulary and all
the verbal gymnastics that make up a song or a poem or
anything. (New York, 1989)

With Joan Baez during the
Rolling Thunder Revue tour, 1976.

Performing

You don't want to just get up there and start guessing
with the people what they want. For one thing, no one agrees
on that. The songs a few people want to hear may not mean
anything to a whole lot of others, and you can't let the audience
start controlling your show or you're going to end up on a
sinking ship. You've got to stay in control, or you might as well
go hole up in Las Vegas somewhere because you're not being
true to the music any more... you're being true to something
else that doesn't really mean anything except some applause.
(Jerusalem, 1987)

What I do is more of an immediate thing. You stand up
on the stage and sing - you get it back immediately. It's not
like writing a book or even making a record ... What I do is so
immediate it changes the nature, the concept, of the art to me.
(New York, 1981)

I always thought that one man, the one balladeer with guitar
could blow an entire army off the stage if he knew what he was
doing. (New York, 1985)

I always play as if nobody out there has ever heard of me.
If you don't do that, you get too complacent and you can't read
a crowd. You start assuming too many things.
(New York, 1989)

Who actually applauds this kind of bullshit.
(London, 1965)

Rolling Thunder Revue

We were all very close. We had this fire going ten years ago
and now we've got it burning again. (Plymouth, Mass, 1975)

That tour was always intended to be a movie. It always existed
on more than one level. That's why the costumes, all the make-
up, something to make it a little more different, to put it in a
time setting, of which the movie would seem to revolve around.
(New York, 1985)

albums

Every time you make an album, you want it to be new, good and different, but personally, when you look back on them - for me - all my albums are just measuring points for whatever I was at a certain period of time. (Malibu, 1978)

Do you listen to your albums?

No, I really don't. I overhear them sometimes when other people have them on, but I don't listen to them. I don't listen to anybody's albums really. Most records - new records - you buy, check them out, see what somebody's doing. But as for sitting down and needing to hear it, y'know, time and time again, throughout your day and night just to feel connected to something, I don't hear nothing around like that these days. I mean for me you know. Other people may find for them those things do that. (Toronto, 1986)

It's one thing to say, 'There's a new record out and responding to the new songs', which is encouraging. But that's not the case. There's no new album, and it's hard for me to know just what that means, why people come out and what they are looking for or listening for... maybe the same things I was looking for when I wrote them. (Los Angeles, 1991)

After you make so many records and the years kinda just go by, it's like you sometimes... you just don't know any more whether... well, am I doing this because I wanna do it or because you think it's expected of you? (Los Angeles, 1991)

Bob Dylan

There was a violent, angry emotion running through me then. I just played the guitar and harmonica and sang those songs and that was it. Mr Hammond asked me if I wanted to sing any of them over again and I said no. I can't see myself singing the same song twice in a row. That's terrible. (New York, 1963)

I couldn't believe it. I left there and I remember walking out of the studio. I was like on a cloud. It was up on 7th Avenue and when I left I was happening to be walking by a record store. It was one of the most thrilling moments in my life. I couldn't believe that I was staring at all the records in the window, Frankie Laine, Frank Sinatra, Patti Page, Mitch Miller, Tony Bennett and so on and so I, myself, would be among them in

the window. I guess I was pretty naïve, you know. It was even before I made a record, just knowing I was going to make one and be in that window... I didn't know that just because you make a record it has to be displayed in a window next to Frank Sinatra, let alone they have to carry it in the store. John Hammond recorded me soon after that.
(New York, 1985)

I just took in what I had. I tried a bunch of stuff and John Hammond would say, 'Well, let's use this one' and I'd sing that one and he'd say, 'Let's use that one'. I must have played a whole lot of songs. He kept what he kept, you know. He didn't ask me what I wrote and what I didn't write. I was only doing a few of my own songs back then, anyway. (New York, 1985)

Freewheelin' Bob Dylan

There's too many old-fashioned songs in there, stuff I tried to write like Woody. I'm goin' through changes. Need some more finger-pointin' songs in it, 'cause that's where my head's at right now. (New York, 1963)

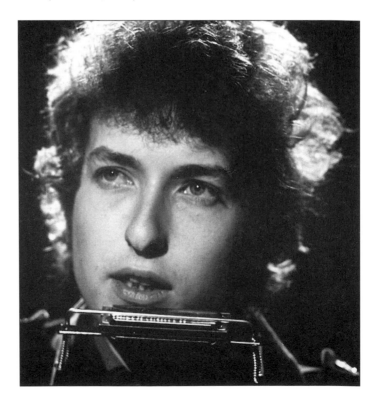

I felt real good about doing an album with my own material. My own material and I picked a little on it. Picked the guitar and it was a big Gibson. I felt real accomplished on that. Got a chance to play in open tuning... 'Oxford Town', I believe that's on the album. That's open tuning. I got a chance to do talking blues. I got a chance to do ballads like 'Girl From The North Country'. It's just because it had more variety. I felt good at that. (New York, 1969)

The Times They Are A-Changin'

When I first started writing those kinds of songs, there wasn't anybody doing things like that. Woody Guthrie had done similar things but he hadn't really done that type of song.
(New York, 1985)

Those songs were all written in the New York atmosphere. I'd never have written any of them - or sung them the way I did - if I hadn't been sitting around listening to performers in New York cafés and the talk in all the dingy parlours. When I got to New York it was obvious that something was going on - folk music - and I did my best to learn and play it. I was just there at the right time with pen in hand. I suppose there was some ambition in what I did. But I tried to make the songs genuine.

Another Side Of Bob Dylan

There aren't any finger-pointin' songs in here... Those records I've made, I'll stand behind them, but some of that was jumping into the scene to be heard and a lot of it was because I didn't see anybody else doing that kind of thing... From now on, I want to write from inside me, and to do that I'm going to have to get back to writing like I used to when I was ten - having everything come out naturally. The way I like to write is for it to come out the way I walk and talk. (New York, 1964)

It's hard being free in a song - getting it all in. Songs are so confining. Woody Guthrie told me once that songs don't have to do anything like that. But it's not true. A song has to have some kind of form to fit into the music. You can bend the words and metre, but it still has to fit somehow. I've been getting freer in the songs I write, but I still feel confined. That's why I write a lot of poetry - if that's the word. Poetry can make its own form. (New York, 1966)

The songs are insanely honest, not meanin' to twist any head and written only for the reason that I myself, me alone, wanted and needed to write them. I've conceded the fact there is no understanding of anything. At best, just winks of the eye and that is all I'm looking for now I guess. (New York, 1964)

I didn't want them to call [my fourth album] 'Another Side of Bob Dylan'... because I thought it was just too corny... I just felt trouble coming when they titled it that. I figured if they could have titled it something else, I wouldn't have had the resistance to it. (Malibu, 1978)

Tom Wilson, the producer, titled it that - I begged and pleaded with him not to do it. You know, I thought it was over-stating the obvious. I knew I was going to have to take a lot of heat for a title like that and it was my feeling that it wasn't a good idea after 'The Times They Are A-Changin',' it just wasn't right. It seemed like a negation of the past which in no way was true. I know that Tom didn't mean it that way, but that's what I figured that people would take it to mean, but Tom meant well and he had control, so he had his way. I guess in the long run, he might have been right to do what he did. It doesn't matter now. (New York, 1985)

Bringing It All Back Home

My old songs, they were what I call one-dimensional songs, but my new songs I'm trying to make more three dimensional, you know. There's more symbolism, they're written on more than one level. (Sheffield, 1965)

Highway 61 Revisited

I'm not gonna be able to make a record better than that one. 'Highway 61' is just too good. There's a lot of stuff on there that I would listen to. (1966)

Blonde On Blonde

You've more space in Nashville than you do in New York. In Nashville people sit around if they want to. If they want to make good records they just sit around and wait all night 'til you're ready. But they won't do that in New York. (New York, 1966)

In 'Blonde On Blonde' I wrote out all the songs in the studio.
The musicians played cards, I wrote out a song, we'd do it, they'd
go back to their game and I'd write out another song.
(New York, 1968)

I was going at a tremendous speed... at the time of my
'Blonde On Blonde' album. (New York, 1969)

The closest I ever got to the sound I hear in my mind was
on individual bands in the 'Blonde On Blonde' album. It's that
thin, that wild mercury sound. It's metallic and bright gold,
with whatever that conjures up. That's my particular sound.
I haven't been able to succeed in getting it all the time.
Mostly I've been driving at a combination of guitar,
harmonica and organ. (New York, 1978)

John Wesley Harding

We recorded that album, and I didn't know what to make
of it. Lots of times people will get excited and say, 'This is great,
this is fantastic'. But usually they're full of shit. They're just
trying to tell you something to make you feel good. People have
a way of telling you what they think you want to hear - any time
I don't know something and I ask somebody, I usually know
less about it after I ask than before. You've got to know or you
don't know and I really didn't know about that album at all.
So I figured the best thing to do would be to put it out as quickly

as possible, call it 'John Wesley Harding' because that was one song I had no idea what it was about, why it was even on the album. I figured I'd call the album that, call attention to it, make it something special... the spelling on that album, I just thought that was the way he spelled his name. I asked Columbia to release it with no publicity and no hype because this was the season of hype. And my feeling was that if they put it out with no hype, there was enough interest in the album anyway, people would go out and get it. And if you hyped it, there was always the possibility it would piss people off. They didn't spend money advertising the album and the album just really took off. People have made a lot out of it, as if it was some sort of ink blot test or something. But it never was intended to be anything else but just a bunch of songs, really, maybe it was better'n I thought. (New York, 1985)

I heard the sound that Gordon Lightfoot was getting, with Charlie McCoy and Kenny Buttrey. I'd used Charlie and Kenny both before, and I figured if he could get that sound, I could. But we couldn't get it. (Woodstock, 1969)

'John Wesley Harding' was a fearful album - just dealing with fear, but dealing with the devil in a fearful way, almost. All I wanted to do was get the words right. (New York, 1978)

There's only two songs on the album which came at the
same time as the music. The rest of the songs were written out
on paper, and I found the tunes for them later. I didn't do it
before, and I haven't done it since. That might account for
the specialness of that album. (Malibu, 1978)

Nashville Skyline

They are the songs I've been writing over the past year.
Some are songs that I've sung and never written down and just
sort of turn up again. I can't remember where they come from.
I was just sitting down trying to write some notes on where the
songs came from and I couldn't figure it out myself.
(New York, 1969)

The first time I went into the studio I had, I think, four songs.
I pulled that instrumental one out... then Johnny [Cash] came in
and did a song with me. Then I wrote one in the motel... pretty
soon the whole album started fillin' in together, and we had an
album. I mean, we didn't go down with that in mind.
(New York, 1969)

These are the types of songs that I always felt like writing
when I've been alone to do so. The songs reflect more of the
inner me than the songs of the past. They're more to my base
than say, 'John Wesley Harding'. There I felt everyone expected
me to be a poet so that's what I tried to be... [My old] songs
were all written in the New York atmosphere. I'd never written
any of them - or sung them in the way I did - if I hadn't been
sitting around listening to performers in New York cafés
and the talk in all the dingy parlours. (New York, 1969)

I like 'Tell Me That It Isn't True', although it came out
completely different than I'd written it. It came out real slow
and mellow. I had it written as a sort of jerky, kind of polka-type
thing. I wrote it in F. That's what gives it a kind of a new sound.
They're all in F... not all of them, quite a few. There's not many
on that album that aren't in F. So you see I had those chords...
which gives it a certain sound. I try to be a little different on
every album. (New York, 1969)

On 'Nashville Skyline' you had to read between the lines. I was
trying to grasp [for] something that would lead me on to where
I thought I should be, and it didn't go nowhere - it just went
down, down, down. I couldn't be anybody but myself, and at that
point I didn't know it or want to know it. (New York, 1978)

With Levon Helm and Rick Danko

Self Portrait

'Self Portrait' was a bunch of tracks we'd done all the time
I'd gone to Nashville. We did that stuff to get a [studio] sound.
To open up we'd do two or three songs, just to get things right
and then we'd go on and do what we were going to do. And then
there was a lot of other stuff that was worse than appearing on
bootleg records. So I just figured I'd put all this stuff together
and put it out, my own bootleg record, so to speak. You know,
if it actually had been a bootleg record, people probably would
have sneaked around to buy it and played it for each other
secretly. Also, I wasn't going to be anybody's puppet and I
figured this record would put an end to that... I was just so
fed up with all the people who thought I was nonsense.
(New York, 1985)

That album was put out... [because] at that time... I didn't
like the attention I was getting. I [had] never been a person
that wanted attention. And at that time I was getting the wrong
kind of attention, for doing things I'd never done. So we
released that album to get people off my back. They would not
like me any more. That's... the reason that album was put out,
so that people would just at that time stop buying my records,
and they did. (New York, 1981)

I feel I have an obligation to my record contract.
This means recording the best songs I can. That's why I look
around for other people's songs. (Woodstock, 1969)

With George Harrison at the Concert for Bangla Desh, 1971.

I said, 'Well, fuck it. I wish these people would just forget about me. I wanna do something they can't possibly like, they can't relate to'... and I did this portrait for the cover. I mean... there was no title for that album, and I said, 'Well, I'm gonna call this album 'Self Portrait'' and to me it was a joke. (1984)

New Morning

We had a few tracks for 'New Morning' before that 'Self Portrait' LP came out. I didn't say, 'Oh my God, they don't like this, let me do another one'. It wasn't like that. It just happened coincidentally that one came out and the other one did as soon as it did. The 'Self Portrait' LP laid around for, I think, a year. We were working on 'New Morning' when the 'Self Portrait' album got put together. Some of that stuff (on 'Self Portrait') was left over from 'Nashville Skyline'.

There was a play on Broadway and a producer got hold of me. He wanted me to write some songs for an Archibald MacLeish play, and it was called *The Devil And Daniel Webster*, so I recorded some stuff based on what he was doing. I recorded 'New Morning', 'Time Passes Slowly' and 'Father Of Night'. So I went up to see Archibald MacLeish with the songs, and with the producer. He lived in Connecticut. Played him the songs and he liked them all. He thought they would fit perfectly until we got to 'Father Of Night'. We didn't see eye to eye on that one so I backed out of the production. It was nothing really, kind of like a misunderstanding I suppose. Anyway, I took those songs and some others and recorded 'New Morning'. (New York, 1985)

Pat Garrett & Billy The Kid

Rudy [Wurlitzer] needed a song for the script. I wasn't doing anything. Rudy sent the script, and I read it and liked it and we got together and he needed a title song. (New York, 1975)

Dylan

I didn't think it was that bad really.
(Montreal, 1974)

Before The Flood

It wasn't a tour where a bunch of guys get together and say, 'Let's go out and play'. There was a great demand for that tour and it had been building up, so we went out and did it. We hadn't made any records. (1989)

Blood On The Tracks

A lot of people tell me they enjoy that album. It's hard for me to relate to that... I mean, it, you know, people enjoying the type of pain, you know? (New York, 1975)

Dylan fronts the Rolling Thunder Revue
in 1976. Former chief Byrd Roger McGuinn
is on the far left.

Everybody agrees that was pretty different. What's different
about it is that there's a code in the lyrics, and there's also no
sense of time. There's no respect for it. You've got yesterday,
today and tomorrow all in the same room, and there's very little
you can't imagine not happening. (New York, 1978)

'Blood On The Tracks' did consciously what I used to do
unconsciously. I didn't perform it well. I didn't have the power
to perform it well. But I did write the songs... the songs that have
the break-up of time, where there is no time, trying to make the
focus as strong as a magnifying glass under the sun. To do that
consciously is a trick, and I did it on 'Blood On The Tracks'
for the first time. I knew how to do it because of a technique
I learned - actually I had a teacher for it ... (New York, 1978)

I was fighting sentimentality all the way down the line.
(Augusta, 1978)

I had a few weeks in the summer when I wrote the songs
for 'Blood On The Tracks' and then I recorded them.
(New York, 1985)

I was just trying to make it like a painting where you can see
the different parts, but then you also see the whole of it.
(New York, 1985)

'Blood On The Tracks' was another one of those records we
went in and did in three or four days... I thought the songs could
have sounded differently, better, so I went in and re-recorded
them. (New York, 1985)

A lot of people thought ... that album, 'Blood On The Tracks'
pertained to me. (New York, 1985)

The Basement Tapes

[The songs] were written vaguely for other people... I don't
remember anybody specifically those songs were ever written
for. They must have been written at that time for the publishing
company... We must have recorded fifty songs at that place.
At that time psychedelic rock was overtaking the universe and
so we were singing those home spun ballads or whatever
they were. (New York, 1978)

Desire

That was new. I didn't take that out as far as I wanted
to, I didn't have the chance to do that. I wanted to do more
harmonica and violin together but we never got a chance to
do that. (Los Angeles, 1978)

I never slept when I made that album, I couldn't sleep.
(Los Angeles, 1978)

We had tried it with a lot of different people in the studio,
a lot of different types of sound, and I even had back-up singers
on that album for two or three days, a lot of percussion, a lot
going on. But as it got down, I got more irritated with all this
sound going on and eventually just settled on bass, drums
and violin. (New York, 1978)

Bob Dylan At Budokan

They twisted my arm to do a live album for Japan. It was
the same band I used on 'Street Legal', and we had just started
findin' our way into things on that tour when they recorded it.
I never meant for it to be any type of representation of my
stuff or my band or my live show. (Los Angeles, 1984)

Street Legal

The critics treated this record spitefully... I saw one review that
accused me of going to 'Vegas' and copying Bruce Springsteen
because I was using Steve Douglas, a saxophone player... the
Vegas comparison was, well you know, I don't think the guy had
ever been to Vegas and the saxophone thing was almost sland-
erous... I mean I don't copy guys that are under fifty years old.
Though I wasn't familiar with Bruce's work, his saxophone player
couldn't be spoken of in the same breath as Steve Douglas who'd
played with Duane Eddy and on literally all of Phil Spector's
records... I mean no offence to Clarence or anything, but he's
not in the same category and the guy who reviewed my stuff
should have known it... anyway, people need to be encouraged,
not stepped on and put in a strait jacket. (New York, 1985)

It took us a week to make 'Street Legal'. We mixed it the
following week and put it out the week after. If we hadn't done
it that fast we wouldn't have made an album at all, because we
were ready to go back on the road. (New York, 1978)

Slow Train

The songs that I wrote for the 'Slow Train' album [frightened me]... I didn't plan to write them, but I wrote them anyway. I didn't like writing them, I didn't want to write them... But I found myself writing these songs and after I had a certain amount of them I thought I didn't want to sing them, so I had a girl sing them for me... A girl I was singing with at the time, Carolyn Denis... I [would give] them all to her and [have] her record them, and not even put my name on them. I wanted the songs out but I didn't want to do it [myself] because I knew that it wouldn't be perceived in that way. It would just mean more pressure. I just did not want to write at that time.
(New York, 1984)

Saved

'Slow Train' was a big album. 'Saved' didn't have those kinda numbers but to me it was just as big an album. I'm fortunate that I'm in a position to release an album like 'Saved' with a major record company so that it will be available to the people who would like to buy it. (New York, 1981)

People didn't like those tunes, they rejected all that stuff when my show would be all off the new album. People would shout, 'We want to hear the old songs.' You know... at a certain point it doesn't really matter any more.
(Los Angeles, 1991)

With Ronnie Wood during Dylan's disastrous Live Aid peformance, 1985.

With Patti Smith.

Shot Of Love

People didn't listen to that album in a realistic way. First of
all, 'Shot Of Love' was one of the last songs Bumps Blackwell
produced, and even though he only produced one song I gotta
say that of all the producers I ever used, he was the best, the
most knowledgeable and he had the best instincts ... I would
have liked him to do the whole thing but things got screwed up
and he wasn't so-called 'contemporary'... what came out was
something close to what would have come out if he was
really there. (New York, 1985)

The record had something that could have been made in the
Forties or maybe the Fifties ... there was a cross element of songs
on it ... the critics ... all they talked about was Jesus this and Jesus
that, like it was some king of Methodist record.
(New York, 1985)

Infidels

Somehow, I figured I could always get away with just
playing the songs live in the studio and leaving. It got to the
point where I felt people expected that from me. But I decided
[on 'Infidels'] to take my time like other people do.
(New York, 1983)

We didn't really approach ['Infidels'] any differently than
any other record. We put the tracks down and sang most of the
stuff live. Only later when we had so much stuff, we recorded
it over [again] ... I wanted to fill it up more, I've never wanted to
do that with any other record ... Did you ever listen to an Eagles
record? ... their songs are good, but every note is predictable,
you know exactly what's gonna be before it's even there. And I

started to sense some of that on 'Infidels', and I didn't like it,
so we decided to re-do some of the vocals ... [But] that record's
not an overly produced record.
(New York, 1984)

Empire Burlesque

What I do now is record all the time. Some times nothing
comes out and other times I get a lot of stuff that I keep.
I recorded ['Empire Burlesque'] for a long time. I just put
down the songs as I felt I wanted to put them down, then listen
and decide if I liked them. And if I didn't like them I'd either re-
record them or change something about them.
(New York, 1985)

I'm the final judge of what goes on and off my records.
This last record I just did, 'Empire Burlesque', there were nine
songs I knew belonged on it, and I needed a tenth. I had about
four songs, and one of those was going to be the tenth song.
I finally figured out that the last song needed to be acoustic,
so I just wrote it. I wrote it because none of the other songs
fit that spot, that certain place.
(New York, 1985)

Biograph

There's some stuff that hasn't been heard before, but most of
my stuff has already been bootlegged, so to anybody in the know,
there's nothing on it they haven't heard before... All it is, really,
is repackaging, and it'll just cost a lot of money.
(New York, 1985)

Down In The Groove

There's no rule that claims that anyone must write their
own songs. And I do. I write a lot of songs. But so what, you know?
You could take another song somebody else has written and
make it yours. I'm not saying I made a definitive version of
anything with this last record, but I liked the songs. Every so
often you've gotta sing songs that're out there... Writing is such
an isolated thing. You're in such an isolated frame of mind.
You have to get into or be in that place. In the old days, I could
get to it real quick. I can't get to it like that no more.
(Los Angeles, 1988)

Oh Mercy

Most of [the songs on 'Oh Mercy'] are stream-of-consciousness
songs, the kind that come to you in the middle of the night,
when you just want to go back to bed.
(New York, 1989)

Some people quit making records. They just don't care about
it any more. As long as they have their live stage show together,
they don't need records. It was getting to that point for me.
It was either come up with a bunch of songs that were original
and pay attention to them or get some other real good songwriters to write me some songs. I couldn't find any other
songs. (New York, 1989)

Could 'Oh Mercy' be described as a bleak record?

It could but then again it needn't be. A lot of that might have to
do with the different textures of instrumentation on it rather
than the songs themselves.

Whose idea were the crickets on 'Man In The Long Black Coat'?

It wasn't my idea!
(New York, 1989)

Bono had heard a few of [my new] songs and suggested that
Daniel Lanois could really record them right. Daniel came to see
me when we were playing in New Orleans last year and... we hit it
off. He had an understanding of what my music was all about.
It's very hard to find a producer that can play... It was thrilling to
run into Daniel because he's a competent musician and he
knows how to record with modern facilities. For me, that was
lacking in the past. (New York, 1989)

*Did you discuss the lyrics with Daniel? Would he ask what certain
sections were about? Would he need to know that to help create an
atmosphere?*

We didn't really do that. Some songs might have had more
lyrics than necessary and he might have said which verse to keep,
maybe whole verses. Generally there weren't too many problems
in the lyrics. It was more ... in fact there wasn't any problem
with them at all. (New York, 1989)

Daniel just allowed the record to take place any old time,
day or night. You don't have to walk through secretaries, pin-
ball machines and managers and hangers-on in the lobby and
parking lots and elevators and arctic temperatures. You need
help to make a record, in all the directions that go into making
a record. Some people expect me to bring in a Bob Dylan song,
sing it and they record it. Other people don't work that way -
there's more feedback. (New York, 1989)

Under The Red Sky

*Does the album title 'Under The Red Sky' refer to the current war
in the Middle East?*

No, not really. The record was released before the hostilities
began. But it's relevant, I'd say. But so are the songs I wrote
thirty years ago. (Guadalajara, Mexico, 1991)

The Traveling Wilburys:
Dylan, Jeff Lynne, Tom Petty, Roy Orbison
and George Harrison.

The Traveling Wilburys
Volume One

It wasn't that difficult to make that record. There weren't really a lot of heavy decisions that went into it. Co-operation is great on something like that because you never get stuck.
(New York, 1989)

[That] was a pretty rushed affair. A lot of stuff was scraped up from jam tapes. (New York, 1990)

Volume Three

There's no telling what kind of record we could have made with Roy [Orbison]. Everyone missed him, but it wasn't like anyone sat around and talked about it.
(New York, 1990)

The songs are more developed. If people liked the first one they'll love this one. (New York, 1990)

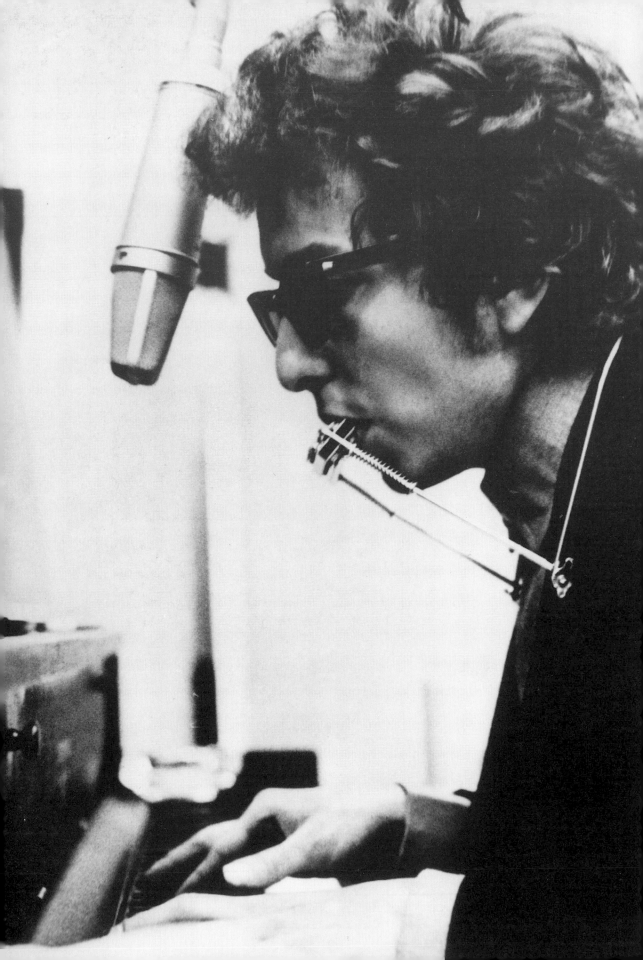

recording

The stuff usually doesn't get onto a record for one of two reasons. Either there's too much on the record, and you can't get the song on it ... or else you just don't think the song is good enough. A lot of stuff I've left off my records I just haven't felt has been good enough. Or maybe it didn't sound like a record to me. (New York, 1985)

You need help to make a record, in all the decisions that go into making a record. People expect me to bring in a Bob Dylan song, sing it, and then record it. Other people don't work that way. There's more feedback. (*USA Today*, 1989)

You were talking about doing your songs differently in concerts...

You know why that happens? It's because a lot of times my records were made... especially in the Seventies... I took a lot of songs into the studio that I wasn't really familiar with. I just had written them, so I didn't know,,, and it depends on what musicians you have playing with you - like what they can do, you know? And sometimes I've been into the studio with bands - just studio guys that have been put together - and you have to figure out which way this band's gonna play, especially if you want to do six songs in a session.

You like to get it over and done with, don't you? You don't want to spend a year doing an album, like some of these other stars now do...

I wouldn't mind spending a year on an album, I mean, if it was worth my while.

Worth your while?

If somebody said to me to try to do a certain thing that took a year or something like that. I don't know why you'd spend a year on an album. I guess you could go off to Rio for part of the time, y'know, record down there, then go to Montserrat, record there, and then maybe take a quick ride to Paris, record there for a couple of weeks... I don't know how you'd spend a year on an album. How's it done? I don't know.

To get it right?

Well, that must be the reason! To get it right. I always figure it can always be more right, so you can always wonder about that. I know I have. (Toronto, 1986)

You didn't get a lot of studio time then. Six months to make a record... It wasn't conceivable. My early records all the way up to the late Seventies, were done in periods of hours. Days, maybe.

Martin Scorcese, Lou Reed, Ian Hunter, Judy Collins, Dylan and Arthur Baker.

Since the late Sixties, maybe since 'Sergeant Pepper' on, everybody started to spend more of their time in the studio, actually making songs up and building them in the studio. I've done a little bit of that but I'd rather have some kind of song before I get there. It just seems to work out better that way. (New York, 1985)

Your albums are a little more produced these days than they used to be?

If that's what you call it.

Do you still use the same recording technique?

Oh, I'd say over the course of a year, maybe a period of six days in the studio, that's probably it. If I can't make a record in six days I don't.

That's the way it's always been, basically?

Yeah. (San Francisco, 1980)

Has [recording] often been a painful experience?

You usually work with people who don't..., with me anyway... you fall into working with people who for one reason or another happen to be there but don't have a great understanding of what it is that you're trying to do. They might know your name and they might know some of the songs but they don't really have a great understanding and the heart to be able to get under it and push it up and make something out of it. They'd rather say, Well show it to me and let's record it and let me think what else I can put on it. (New York, 1989)

Changes Record Label

It was long overdue. Just a feeling that it was time to go on... suspected (CBS) were doing more talk than action. Just released them and that's all. Got a feeling they didn't care whether I stayed or not. (1974)

Videos

I'm not quite sure I know what a video is except that the market for video is new, but the form has always been there. Yeah, [they view] 'Subterranean Homesick Blues' as a video. I don't know if it was a video. We didn't think of it as a video at the time, we just needed a piece of film to go at the beginning of the movie ... We wanted to do 'Neighbourhood Bully' but [it's difficult] tryin' to explain to somebody what you see and drawin' up storyboards. I haven't really found anybody that really thinks a certain way that needs to be [done], like the German film-makers, the English film-makers. In the States there aren't people like that. They just don't exist ... I visualised 'Neighbourhood Bully' ... there were certain segments which I just wrote down one night which I thought would look great on film and it would be like a Fassbinder movie.
(Los Angeles, 1984)

Over page:
With Robbie Robertson of the Band.

films & books

Do you have any future movie plans?

Yeah, I have plans to make a movie with Alan Rudolph next fall.

With who?

Alan Rudolph. He's a movie director. He's a bright guy.
It's a complicated story, about a piano player who gets into
trouble because of a good buddy of his, and then he winds
up doing some book work for a woman whose husband has
disappeared, marries her, then falls in love with her daughter.
And the other guy finally shows up again and the movie comes
to a screaming halt. (Toronto, 1986)

My lawyer used to tell me there was a future in movies. So I said,
'What kind of future?' He said, 'Well, if you can come up with a
script, an outline and get money from a big distributor', but I
knew I couldn't work that way. I can't betray my vision on a little
piece of paper in hopes of getting some money from somebody.
In the final analysis, it turned out that I had to make the movie
all by myself, with people who would work with me, who trusted
me. I went on the road in '76 to make money for this movie.
(New York, 1978)

For me, film wouldn't be the right thing to do right now.
It's not live enough. You're acting for a camera, a director, you
can't really see the results. (New York, 1979)

It costs too much money for one, to make your own movie, and
then if you make a movie for another man who's putting up the
money, then he'll want what he wants.
(New York, 1979)

Tarantula

I have a lot of words written for it but I can't use anything
I've written... before a year ago... I can't really use the ideas.
They're so deformed and just not really right ideas. Stuff which
has been expressed a million times in the past... I don't write
now unless it just happens. (Detroit, 1965)

[The working title is] tentatively, 'Bob Dylan Off The
Record.' But they tell me there's already books out with that
'off the record' title. The book can't really be titled, that's the
kind of book it is. I'm also going to write the reviews for it...

Opposite: The cast of *Hearts Of Fire*;
Rupert Everett, Fiona Flanagan, Dylan.

I've written some songs which are kind of far out, a long
continuation of verses, stuff like that... I haven't really gotten
into writing a completely free song. You dig something like cut-
ups?... I wrote the book because there's a lot of stuff in there I
can't possibly sing... Something that has no rhyme, all cut up,
no nothing except something happening which is words.
(Santa Monica, 1965)

I just put down all these words and sent them off to my
publishers and they'd send back the galleys, and I'd be so
embarrassed at the nonsense I'd written I'd change the whole
thing. And all the time they had 100,000 orders... The trouble
with it, it had no story. I'd been reading all these trash books,
works suffering from sex and excitement and foolish things.
(Woodstock, 1968)

It's about spiders... it's an insect book.
(London, 1965)

I'm writing a book now... It's about my first week in New York...
It's just about somebody who's come to the end of one road and
knows it's the end of one road, and knows there's another road
there but doesn't know exactly where it is, and knows you can't
go back on this one road... it's got thoughts in my head all about
teachers and school and all about hitch-hikers around the
country... college kids going to college it's got, and these are all
the people that I knew. Every one of them's sort of a symbol
for all kinds of people. (New York, 1963)

Don't Look Back

You know this movie, *Don't Look Back*. Well that splashed
my face all over the world. I didn't get a penny from that movie,
you know... so when people say why don't you go out and work
and why don't you do this and why don't you do that, people
don't know half of what a lot of these producers and people,
lawyers... they don't know the half of these stories. I'm an easy
going kind of fellow, you know... I forgive and forget. But I'm
not interested in finding out any more about a film.

Robbie Robertson, Rick Danko and
Dylan.

Did you like Don't Look Back?
I'd like it a lot more if I got paid for it.
(New York, October 1969)

Don't Look Back was... somebody else's movie. It was a deal worked
out with a film company, but I didn't really play any part in it.
When I saw it in a movie house, I was shocked at what had been
done. I didn't find out until later that the camera had been on
me all the time. That movie was done by a man who took it
all out of context. It was documented from his personal point
of view. The movie was dishonest, it was a propaganda movie.
I don't think it was accurate at all in terms of showing my
formative years. It showed only one side. He made it seem like
I wasn't doing anything but living in hotel rooms, playing the
typewriter and holding press conferences for journalists.
All that is true, you know. Throwing some bottles, there's
something about it in the movie. Joan Baez is in it. But it's one-
sided. Let's not lean on it too hard. It just wasn't representative
of what was happening in the Sixties. I wasn't really a star in
those days, any more than I'm a star these days. I was very
obviously confused then as to what my purpose was. It was
pretty early, you know. 'The Times They Are A-Changin'' was
on the English charts then, so it had to be pretty early.
(Malibu, 1978)

Have you ever watched Don't Look Back?
Oh many years ago. It's very hard for me to look at anything
that has to do with me. (New York, 1989)

Eat The Document

What we had to work with was not what you would conceive
of if you were going shooting a film. What we were trying to do
was make a logical story out of this newsreel-type footage...
to make a story which consisted of stars and starlets who were
taking the roles of other people, just like a normal movie would
do. We were trying to do the same thing with this footage.
That's not what anyone else had in mind, but that's what myself
and Mr Alk had in mind. And we were very limited because the
film was not shot by us, but by the eye, and we had come upon
this decision to do this only after everything else had failed...
What we tried to do was construct a stage and an environment,
taking it out and putting it together like a puzzle. And we did,
that's the strange part about it. Now if we had the opportunity
to re-shoot the camera under this procedure, we could really
make a wonderful film. (Woodstock, 1968)

Pat Garrett & Billy The Kid

I don't know who I played. I tried to play whoever it was in
the story, but I guess it's a known fact that there was nobody in
that story that was the character I played.
(Montreal, 1974)

I learned by working in Pat Garrett that there is no way you
can make a really creative movie in Hollywood... You have to
have your own crew and your own people to make a movie
your own way. (Malibu, 1978)

That [movie] was Peckinpah's kingdom - and he was sort of a
madman. He kept saying, 'It's my movie, my movie'.
(Los Angeles, 1986)

Sam [Peckinpah] himself just didn't have final control and
that was the problem. I saw it in a movie house one cut away from
his and I could tell that it had been chopped to pieces. Someone
other than Sam had taken a knife to some valuable scenes that
were in it. The music seemed to be scattered and used in every
other place but the scenes that we did it for. Except for 'Heaven's
Door', I can't say as though I recognised anything I'd done [as]...
being in the place I'd done it for. (New York, 1985)

Renaldo & Clara

I knew it was not going to be a short hour movie because we couldn't tell that story in an hour. Originally I couldn't see how we could do it under seven or eight hours. But we subtracted songs and scenes and dialogue until we couldn't subtract any more. (New York, 1978)

Renaldo and Clara was originally intended as a more structured film. I hired playwright Sam Shepard to provide dialogue but we didn't use much of his stuff because of a conflict in ideas. (Malibu, 1978)

There was a lot of chaos while we were making the film. A lot of good scenes didn't happen because we had already finished improvising them by the time the cameras were ready to film. You can't recapture stuff like that. There was a lot of conflict during filming. We had people who didn't understand what we were doing because we didn't have a script. Some who didn't understand were willing to go along with us anyway. Others weren't and that hurt us, and hurt the film. (New York, 1978)

Bob Dylan is being used here as a famous man, so we don't have to hire Marlon Brando!... Let's say that in real life Bob Dylan fixes his name on the public. He can retrieve that name at will. Anything else the public makes of it is its business. (New York, 1977)

Reading the reviews of the movie, I sensed a feeling of them wanting to crush things. Those reviews weren't about the movie. They were just an excuse to get at me for one reason or another... I was disappointed that the critics couldn't get beyond the superficial elements. They thought the movie was all about Bob Dylan, Joan Baez and Sara Dylan... and [it] wasn't. (Los Angeles, 1978)

This is a movie done without a script. There were ideas from the beginning, but a lot of this film developed as we were doing it. Quite a bit was improvised, but only within certain rules. (Los Angeles, 1978)

I'm doing this to put forth a certain vision which I carry around and can't express on any other canvas. (New York, 1978)

The film is no puzzle, it's A-B-C-D, but the composition's
like a game - the red flower, the hat, the red and blue themes.
The interest is not the literal plot but in the associated texture-
colours, images, sounds. (New York, 1977)

The movie creates and holds time. That's what it should do -
it should hold that time, breathe in that time and stop time in
doing that. It's like if you look at a painting by Cézanne, you get
lost in the painting for that period of time. And you breathe - yet
time is going by and you wouldn't know it. You're spellbound.
(New York, 1978)

Do you think that making this film has been a waste of money?

If the film medium is a true canvas then the film has been
worthwhile. (Los Angeles, 1978)

So Bob Dylan may or may not be in the film?

Exactly.

But Bob Dylan made the film.

Bob Dylan didn't make it. I made it.
(New York, 1978)

The whole movie was his [Renaldo's] dream... Renaldo lives
in a tomb, his only way out is to dream.
(New York, 1977)

The film reveals that there's a whole lot to reveal beneath the surface of the soul, but it's unthinkable... It reveals the depths that there are to reveal. And that's the most you can ask, because things are really very invisible... And this film goes as far as one can to reveal that. (New York, 1978)

It's about the essence of man being alienated from himself and how, in order to free himself, to be re-born, he has to go outside himself. You can almost say that he dies in order to look at time, and by strength of will can return to the same body...

What are [Renaldo's] needs?

A good guitar and a dark street.

The guitar because he loves music, but why the dark street?

Because he needs to hide... From the demon within.
But what we all know is that you can't hide on a dark street from the demon within... He tries to escape from the demon within, but he discovers that the demon is, in fact, a mirrored reflection of Renaldo himself. (New York, 1978)

I talked too much about that film already.
(London, 1978)

Clara is the symbol of freedom in this movie. She's what attracts Renaldo at the present. Renaldo lives in a tomb, his only way out is to dream... You know at the end of the movie he's about to, or has broken out of the tomb... you feel that even though he may be under strenuous times, he might transcend them... He's trying to break out of himself... not only that, he's trying to break out of himself by means of reason... he's actually in the process of conquering his own soul... [the end of the movie] is in fact the morning of Renaldo's life. (New York, 1977)

Renaldo has faith in himself and his ability to dream, but the dream is sometimes so powerful it has the ability to wipe him out. Renaldo has no ordinary mind - he might not even have a soul. He may actually be Time itself, in his wildest moments.
(New York, 1977)

Renaldo is everybody... Renaldo is you, struggling within yourself, with the knowledge that you're locked within the chains of your own being... He's Everyman in the movie, and he survives. He is a man contemplating the future... At the beginning of the movie he's in a mask you can see through - it's translucent. At the end he's seen putting on face paint.
(New York, 1977)

Top: *The Hearts Of Fire* cast.
Below: Dylan with Robert De Niro.

Hearts Of Fire

I could never have written a script like this, this is beyond me.
(London, 1986)

Do you think that 'Hearts Of Fire' is the worst rock movie ever to be made?

It could be. Although to me it was never a rock'n'roll movie
anyway. It's too bad it wasn't something more to my liking, like
'Chariots Of Fire'. It's too bad they didn't give me that script...
They paid me as much as they'd probably pay Robert De Niro.
Anybody would have done it.
(Los Angeles, 1990)

So how do you decide which kind of a script attracts you?
Or, why this one?

Because I've got to tell you when I read this script I just
thought... well, as it turns out I can see it's all working, but when
I first read the script, I've got to be honest, I didn't think it
looked too good. Well, I heard that too, you know. I heard that.
But... I don't know. I guess it's better than it looks!
(Toronto, 1986)

You're putting a lot of work and a lot of time into this film, and
then you say you're not going to see it.

Oh I may see it, I might go see it. I don't know. I'm not sure
about the date it's gonna open.

You say it's a joy to work with Fiona [Flanagan], that she's got what it takes.

I think so. I think she could be the next Joan Crawford.

I think I meant as a singer.

I'm talking about acting. As a singer? She could be the next anybody. She don't have to be the next anybody, she could be the first one like her. (Toronto, 1986)

In the words of Billy Parker, 'You wake up you're a star - so, you're a star. But there ain't nothin' to you no more; you're empty.' Is that a sentiment you would agree with?

Well some stars are like that, yeah.

Are you?

No, I'm not like that, but I'm playing another character who is like that. I'm getting into my character right now. (London, 1986)

Bob Dylan's written four songs for this movie. Can you tell me a little bit about them?

Well, I haven't written those songs just yet.

The person that I consulted on it told me that you had.

Well, I'm about to.

What are they going to be about?

They're going to be about the movie.

Are they going to be protest songs?

I hope so, yes.
(London, 1986)

Is there a particular scene in the film...?

Not really, I don't really know the scenes in this movie to tell you the truth. They're all good I guess. I'm a perfectionist maybe in other areas than movie making...
(Bristol, 1986)

When I asked, 'What am I supposed to do in this scene?' the director would say, 'Just be yourself'. Then I'd have to think, 'Which one?' Nobody ever explained that to me.
(Los Angeles, 1990)

You could say that I'm somebody like [Billy] Parker who became famous through music and that I had certain feelings about fame. (London, 1986)

the rock & roll lifestyle

Drugs

It's fine if they use pot and LSD and heroin and sex and everything. I mean that's groovy... To know pot - or to know any drug - is fine, and it's not gonna fuck you up... I mean, LSD is a medicine. You take it and you know... you don't really have to keep taking it all the time.
(New York, 1965)

I wouldn't advise anybody to use drugs - certainly not the hard drugs; drugs are medicine. But opium and hash and pot - now, those things aren't drugs; they just bend your mind a little. I think everybody's mind should be bent once in a while.
(Los Angeles, 1966)

A lot of young people who admire you seem to be mixed-up in a lot of drug-taking. Do you agree with this? What are your views on the problem?

I don't have any views. I sure wish I did ▪ I sure would like to share them with you all. (New York, 1969)

I guess everybody's smoked pot.
(Boston, 1965)

Grass was everywhere in the clubs. It was always there in the jazz clubs, and in the folk-music clubs. There was just grass and it was available to musicians... When psychedelics happened, everything became irrelevant. Because that had nothing to do with making music, or writing poems... People were deluded into thinking they were something they weren't.
(New York, 1978)

Drugs were something that was just a playful thing or something which wasn't romanticised. Drugs were always in the folk clubs and in the jazz clubs, but outside of those places I never really saw too many drugs. The drugs at the end of the Sixties were more artificial. They were those L.S... .acid, all that stuff made in a laboratory. Well I guess it's all made in a laboratory one way or another. I don't know. I was never involved in the acid scene either. (New York, 1979)

You had a drug period at one time didn't you?

I never got hooked on any drug - not like you'd say Eric Clapton did in his drug period.

Ever take LSD?

I don't wanna say anything to encourage anybody, but who knows? Who knows what people stick in your drinks, or what kinda cigarettes you're smokin'?
(Los Angeles, 1984)

Drugs were never that big a thing with me. I could take them or leave them. Never hung me up.
(New York, 1985)

Top: Dylan with Eric Clapton.
Below: With Graham Parker.

Money

If you can work that's all you can ask. In this day and age
you can't take that for granted. Just to be able to work is what
a person should strive after.

*I think I know what you mean, but a lot of people might say it's all very
well for Bob Dylan to say that he's got a whole lot of money.*

Whole lot of money?

You don't need money do you?

I don't need money. Don't talk to me about money. I had
less than anyone I know. I started out with no money. If you're
talking about paper money and money in the bank or value
wealth, possessions and all that stuff, I had nothing, so it's not
like I went out and got into music to make money. There wasn't
any money to be made in music when I started out. If you could
just support yourself you were doing good. There wasn't any
money. It wasn't this big million dollar industry that it is today
and people do go into it just to make money and because it's
proved you can make money in that field, but that's the sad
thing I guess. Because it changes the quality of the work that's
being done and you can tell. If you listen to the popular tastes of
the people what they're being given is a different thing.
(Toronto, 1986)

Money was never a motivation to write anything. I never
wrote anything with 'this is gonna be a big hit or this isn't' type
of attitude. I'm not that smart anyway.
(New York, 1985)

How much money do you have?

I have about 75 million dollars, all sewed into my jacket-lining.
(Stockholm, 1966)

How would you change your life?

How would I change my life? Yeah, well, sometimes I think
that I get by on only fifty percent of what I got, sometimes even
less. I'd like to change that I guess... that's about all I can think of.
(New York, 1985)

With Jack Nicholson.

Top: With Mick Jagger.

Fame

Would you welcome being anonymous again?

Well, I would to a degree, but not really. I wouldn't want to be anybody else except me.

I meant anonymous in the sense that you could walk down the street.

Well, yeah. Anybody would welcome that. That's another thing, but then again being me I can get all sorts of favours from people, y'know. (New York, 1965)

People treat famous people all the same. It doesn't matter what the person's famous for, you could be famous for the shooting of the President or something, you're still famous and they put your picture on all the newspapers. You could be a famous fashion designer or a famous movie star or a famous Wall Street executive, but you're still on your degree of fame. You know you're just famous and people react to famous people so if you talk to famous people, and I guess I am one of them because I have a certain degree of notoriety and fame, and everybody just kinda copes with it in a different way, but nobody really seems to think it's what they went after. A lot of people go after fame and money, but they're really after the money, they don't want the fame... It's like, say you're passing a little pub or an inn, and you look through the window and you

see all the people eating and talking and carrying on, you can
watch outside the window and you can see them all being very
real with each other. As real as they're gonna be, because when
you walk into the room it's over. You won't see them being
real any more. (Toronto, 1986)

I don't pay any attention to it. I just don't. Life is too
short and what do most people want? They want your autograph.
Nobody knows me and I don't know them, y'know. They walk up
and they think they know me because I've written some song that
happens to bother them in a certain way and they can't get rid of
it in their mind. They got nothin' to do with me, they still don't
know me and I still don't know them so they walk up as if we're
long lost brothers or sisters or something. That's got nothin'
to do with me. I think I could prove that in any court.
(Toronto, 1986)

It wasn't me who called myself a legend. It was thrown at me
by editors in the media who wanted to play around with me or
have something new to tell their readers. But it stuck. It was
important for me to come to the bottom of this legend thing,
which has no reality at all. What's important isn't the legend but
the art, the work. A person has to do whatever they are called on
to do. If you try to act the legend, it's nothing but hype.

Many people describe you as a genius.
Genius? That's a real fine line between genius and insanity.
Anybody will tell you that.
(Los Angeles, 1992)

I'm not concerned with the myth, because I can't work under
the myth. The myth can't write the songs. It's the blood behind
the myth that creates the art. The myth doesn't exist for me like
it may for other people. I'd rather go on, above the myth.
(New York, 1977)

It seems funny for me to say, but I don't really care for the
bright lights that much. (San Francisco, 1980)

It's been years since I've read anything about myself.
[People] can think what they want and let me be. You couldn't
let fame get in the way of your calling. Everybody is entitled to
lead a private life. Then again, God watches everybody, so there's
nothing really private, there's nothing we can really hide. As
long as you're exposing everything to the power that created
you, people can't uncover too much.
(Los Angeles, 1979)

*Over the past eighteen years or so you've been written about and
analysed and criticised and second guessed and worshipped by many.
As times goes on does it ever get any easier being Bob Dylan?*

Well, it's easy being Bob Dylan, it's just being, you know, trying
to live up to what people would want Bob Dylan to do that might
be difficult, but it's not really that difficult.

*Is it difficult living up to those expectations? Is it something you've
learned to live with, or is it a burden sometimes?*

As long as I keep it straight in my mind who I am and not
get that confused with who I'm supposed to be, I think I'll be all
right. (San Francisco, 1980)

It's important to stay away from the celebrity trap.
The Andy Warhol-fame-for-a-minute type trip. The media is
a great meat grinder, it's never satisfied and it must be fed but
there's power in darkness too and in keeping things hidden.
Look at Napoleon. Napoleon conquered Europe and nobody
even knew what he looked like... people get too famous too
fast these days and it destroys them
(New York, 1985)

Look at Elvis - he's bigger now than when he was living.
He lives on in people's minds. But you wonder if people are
remembering the right things about his music, rather than
all the stuff people wrote about him.
(Kansas City, 1992)

Top: With David Bowie.
Below: With Julian Lennon.

Fame is a curse. There's a lot of truth in that.

With Joan Baez.

Love

People fall in love with a person's body, with who they know, with the way they dress, with their scorecards. With everything but their real selves, which is what you need to love if you're to be happy together. (1978)

It's like I got enough around me, y'know. So I don't need no people's love. I don't need to go out and play to a crowd of twenty, thirty, fifty thousand people for their love. Some performers have to y'know, but I don't. I've got enough love in my immediate surroundings so I don't care, I don't need... you know what I'm talking about?

I'm fascinated by what you're saying. So that would account for why...

It accounts for why a lot of entertainers do what they do because they want the love of another group of people, y'know. I don't do it for love. I do it because I can do it and I think I'm good at it, that's all I do it for.
(Toronto, 1986)

I am on a sort of crossroads in my life and I can do without love. I can feel the attraction but I can also keep myself apart. I admire beauty more than anything else but now I don't feel I must possess it. The ideal man or woman doesn't exist. When you look for something you are not really looking for a man or a woman. You are looking for someone who awakes something which is buried inside you and once that person does it you become familiar and you always want that and then you stay with that person. But two people who are in love are not in love with just each other. There is a third element intermingled and that third element is an ideal. Both must love the same ideal and that is what they have to share. If that doesn't exist, then it's not love, it's necessity. (Los Angeles, 1989)

Marriage

I'd rather not tell the world why I got married. Even though my ex-wife and I don't have a relationship now, she is still the mother of my children and I see fit to protect her.
(Malibu, 1978)

Marriage was a failure. Husband and wife was a failure, but mother and father wasn't a failure. I wasn't a very good husband. I don't know what a good husband is. I was good in some ways and not so good in other ways.
(New York, 1978)

Divorce

No one in my family gets divorced. It's just unheard of, nobody does that. And so when I did get married I never conceived of getting divorced. I figured it would last forever. But it didn't, and now there's a marriage and there's a divorce. And the circumstances in my life have led to the divorce really being a divorce... most people don't really get divorced. They keep some contact which is great for the kids. But in my case, I first got really married, and then I got really divorced.
(New York, 1978)

religion

People that march with slogans and things tend to make themselves a little too holy. It would be a drag if they, too, started using God as a weapon. (*Playboy*, 1966)

God is a woman... you take it from there.
(Austin, Texas, 1965)

Are you religious?
Well, I don't know, what does that mean, religious. Does it mean you bow down to an idol or go to church every Sunday, that kind of stuff?

Do you believe in something?
No, I don't believe in anything. No, why should I believe in anything. I don't see anything to believe in.

Are you cynical?
No, I'm not cynical. I just can't see anything that anybody's offered me to believe in that I'm gonna believe and put my trust and faith and everything in. Nothing's sacred, man.
(Newcastle-upon-Tyne, 1965)

Did you ever read the Bible?
What about the Bible?

Did you ever read the Bible?
No.

Have you ever read it?
Have I ever? I've glanced through it.

Because a lot of the things you say...
I've glanced through it. I haven't read it.
(London, 1965)

I believe in everything the Bible says.

Do you read the Bible a lot?
Yes.

All the time?
Always.

Which are your favourite books in the Bible?
Leviticus and Deuteronomy.

What do you think about the Apocalypse?

It will not be by water, but by fire next time. It's what is written.

Which edition of the Bible do you read?

The King James's version.

That's not really a Fundamentalist version of the Bible, is it?

I've never been Fundamentalist. I've never been born-again.
Those are just labels that people hang on you. They mean about
as much as Folk Singer, Protest Singer, Rock Star. That's to say
that they don't mean anything at all.
(Budapest, 1991)

Beauty can be very, very deceiving and it's not always of God.
Beauty appeals to our eyes... The beauty of the sunset... that's
God-given. [But] I spent a lot of time dealing with man-made
beauty, so sometimes the beauty of God's world has evaded me.
(New York, 1981)

Religion is another form of bondage which man invents to
get himself to God. But that's why Christ came. Christ didn't
preach religion. He preached the Truth, the Way and the Life.
(Santa Monica, 1979)

Self-righteousness would be just to repeat what you know
has been written down in the scripture some place else. It's not
like you're trying to convince anybody of anything. You're just
saying what the original rule is, and it's coming through you.
But if someone else can get past you saying it and just hear
what the message is, well then it's not coming from you but
through you. And I don't see anything wrong in that.
(New York, 1985)

I was saying stuff I figured people needed to know. I thought
I was giving people an idea of what was behind the songs.
(New York, 1980)

That [born-again period] was all part of my experience.
It had to happen. When I get involved in something, I get totally
involved. I don't just play around on the fringes.
(New York, 1983)

It would have been easier if I'd become a junkie, or a Buddhist
or a Scientologist. (Hartford, Connecticut, 1980)

Whatever label is put on you, the purpose of it is to limit
your accessibility to people. There had been so many labels laid

on me in the past it didn't matter any more at that point. What more could they say? (New York, 1985)

Some critics have not been too kind as a result of the past two albums because of the religious content. Does that surprise you? For example they've said, some have said, that you're proselytizing. Is Jesus Christ the answer for all of us in your mind?

Yeah, I would say that. What we're talking about is the nature of God and in order to go to God you have to go through Jesus. Yeah, you have to understand that. You have to have an experience with that.

You're not preaching to us?

No, I'm not. I could do a little bit of this and a little bit of that but right now I'm just content to play these shows. This is a stage show we're doing. It's not a salvation ceremony.
(San Francisco, 1980)

Sinéad O'Connor lurks in the background during the Dylan 30th Anniversary tribute at Madison Square Garden.

Christianity

Christianity is making Christ the Lord of your life. You're talking about your life now, you're not talking about just part of it, you're not talking about a certain hour every day. You're talking about making Christ the Lord and Master of your life, the King of your life. And you're also talking about Christ, the resurrected Christ. You're not talking about some dead man who had a bunch of good ideas and was nailed to a tree. (Hartford, Connecticut, 1980)

Jesus put his hand on me. It was a physical thing. I felt it. I felt it all over me. I felt my whole body tremble. The glory of the Lord knocked me down and picked me up. (Dayton, Ohio, 1980)

There was a presence in the room that couldn't have been anybody but Jesus... I truly had a born again experience, if you want to call it that. (Dayton, Ohio, 1980)

All these sad stories that are floating around. We're not worried about any of that - we don't care about the atom bomb, any of that, 'cause we know this world is going to be destroyed and Christ will set up His kingdom in Jerusalem for a thousand years, where the lion will lie down with the lamb. (San Francisco, 1979)

There are only two kinds of people. There's saved people and there's lost people... Jesus is Lord and every race shall bow to Him! (Tempe Gammage, 1979)

You may have your college education to hang on to now, but you're gonna need something very solid to hang on to when these [end] days come. (Tempe Gammage, 1979)

Christ is no religion... [He] is the way, the truth and the life... religion is another form of bondage that man invents to get himself to God. (Tucson, 1979)

The world as we know it is being destroyed. Sorry, but it's
the truth. In a short time - I don't know, in three years, maybe
five years, could be ten years, I don't know- there's gonna be
a war. It's gonna be called the War of Armageddon... As sure
as you are standing there, it's gonna happen.
(Santa Monica, 1979)

Walking with Jesus is no easy trip, but it's the only trip.
(Hartford, 1980)

I follow God, so if my followers are following me, indirectly
they're gonna be following God too, because I don't sing any
song which hasn't been given to me by the Lord to sing.
(New York, 1979)

My ideology now would be coming out of the scripture.
Y'see I didn't invent these things - these things have been shown
to me. I'll stand on that faith - that they are true. I believe they're
true. I know they're true.
(Tucson, 1979)

I know the modern trend. It's not fashionable to think
about heaven and hell. I know that. But God doesn't have to
be in fashion. He's always fashionable. But it's hard not to go to
hell, you know. There's so many distractions, so many influences.
You start walking right and pretty soon there's somebody out
there gonna drag you down. As soon as you get rid of The
Enemy outside, The Enemy comes inside. He got all kinds of
ways. The Bible says, 'Resist the Devil and the Devil will flee.'
You got to stand to resist him. How we got to stand? Anybody
know how to stand? How do we stand? Anybody know how?
(muted response from the audience). We gotta stay here
and play another night. (Hartford, 1980)

Judaism

I don't really consider myself Jewish or non-Jewish... I'm not
a patriot to any creed. I believe in all of them and none of them.
A devout Christian or Moslem can be just as effective as a
devout Jew. (Los Angeles, 1978)

My so-called Jewish roots are in Egypt. They went down there
with Joseph, and they came back out with Moses, you know, the
guy that killed the Egyptian, married an Ethiopian girl and
brought the law down from the mountain. The same Moses
whose staff turned into a serpent. The same person who killed
three hundred thousand Hebrews for getting down, stripping
off their clothes and dancing around a golden calf... Roots,
man - we're talking about Jewish roots, you want to know more?
Check up on Elijah the prophet. He could make it rain.
Isaiah the prophet, even Jeremiah - see if their brethren didn't
want to bust their brains for telling it right like it is, yeah - these
are my roots, I suppose.

Are you looking for them?

Am I looking for them? Well, I don't know. I ain't looking for
them in synagogues with six pointed Egyptian stars shining down
from every window, I can tell you that much.
(Minneapolis, 1983)

music

If you want to find out anything that's happening now, you have to listen to the music. I don't mean the words... You gotta listen to The Staples Singers, Smokey & The Miracles, Martha & The Vandellas. That's scary to a lot of people. It's sex that's involved. (New York, 1965)

Popular songs are the only art form that describes the temper of the times... that's where people hang out. It's not in books; it's not on the stage; it's not in the galleries.
(New York, 1965)

You've always done your own thing, back when The Beatles did 'Sergeant Pepper' and The Rolling Stones did 'Satanic Majesties', you came out with 'John Wesley Harding' which was totally different, against the grain of the psychedelic thing.

I wasn't going in the direction of that type of thing... I never was. I tried to keep my music simple. (San Francisco, 1980)

The kids [today] are getting a raw deal. Nobody's telling them anything through music any more. They're just getting a lot of consumer products that aren't doing them any good at all. Sooner or later, they're going to rebel against it all. They don't need to follow me. They have their own people to follow.
(Los Angeles, 1985)

Can you say a bit more about the sort of music that people are being fed out of what they suppose is this vast money orientated industry?

Well, it's about to change, it will change. Machines are making most of the music now. Have you noticed that all songs sound the same? I mean I don't know if you've noticed that. You can be hearing one song and you could take the lyrics of another song and put it right into it because the rhythms are the same and the drums are the same and the machines can only do so much and they can only make it sound different so many different kinds of ways so it doesn't sound different, it sounds all the same. And now that's good for the industry because a lot of people invent these machines and need to sell these machines, plus it's also very good because a person now, the good things you can do with them. You can have your own little band, like a one man band with these machines. You know what I mean? But that's not the point. The point really isn't to be a one man band unless you can play an instrument like a one man band, y'know. I remember Roger McGuinn, years ago he used to take a tape recorder on stage, long before synthetic music became popular, and he used to play the background track from one of his songs and he'd stand there and sing it. I think he was probably the first person ever to do that but that type of music doesn't have any kind of foundation to it, you see. And then there's a lot of kids all around and they just don't like it, so what they're doing they're just buying instruments and playing but they're not listening to those records either, they're listening to the old records so there's a lot of young groups and a lot of young kids that are playing music which I see that play the old style of music. And they're all kids now, but in four or five years they won't be and it's all gonna turn around. That's the way I see it anyway.

Will that be good?

Yeah because... no, there are certain rules and regulations to it, I mean you just don't sit down and write a song. There's a certain amount of learning you have to go through to get to that point and not only living experience, you also have to learn how to play an instrument and carry some kind of tune, I guess. So yeah, that is gonna be good. (Toronto, 1987)

We were recording something the other night and we were gonna put some hand claps on it. And the guy sitting behind the board, he was saying, 'Well do you guys wanna go out there and actually clap? I got a machine right here that can do that.' We went out and clapped instead... But that's just a small example of how everything is just machine orientated. (Los Angeles, 1984)

Nothing is new. Everybody just gets their chance - most of it
sounds recycled and shuffled around, watered down. Even rap
records. I love that stuff but it's not new, you need to hear that
stuff all the time... there was this one guy, Big Brown, he wore a
jail blanket, that's all he ever used to wear, summer and winter,
John Hammond would remember him too - he was like Othello,
he'd recite epics like some grand Roman orator, really backwater
stuff though, Stagger Lee, Cocaine Smitty, Hattiesburg Hattie.
Where were the record companies when he was around?
Even him though, it's like it was done thirty years before
that... and God knows when else. (New York, 1985)

*Do you think that you've played any role in the change of popular
music in the last few years?*

I hope not.
(Woodstock, 1969)

All you heard [back in the late Fifties] was rock & roll
and country & western and rhythm & blues music. Now, at a
certain time the whole field got taken over into some milk, you
know - into Frankie Avalon, Fabian and this kind of thing...
So everybody got out of it. And I remember when everybody got
out of it. But nobody really lost that whole thing. And then folk
music came in as some kind of substitute for a while, but it was
only a substitute... Now it's different again, because of the
English thing... What the English thing did was, they proved that
you could make money at playing the same old kind of music
that you used to play. (Los Angeles, 1966)

Rock & Roll

The thing about rock & roll is that for me anyway it wasn't enough, 'Tutti Frutti' and 'Blue Suede Shoes' were great catch phrases and driving pulse rhythms and you could get high on the energy but they weren't serious or didn't reflect life in a realistic way. I knew when I got into folk music, it was more of a serious type of thing. The songs are filled with more despair, more sadness, more triumph, more faith in the supernatural, much deeper feelings... There is more real life in one line than there was in all the rock & roll themes. I needed that. Life is full of complexities and rock & roll didn't reflect that. It was just put on a happy face and ride Sally ride, there was nothing even resembling 'Sixteen Snow White Horses' or 'See That My Grave Is Kept Clean' in even the vaguest way. If I did anything, I brought one to the other. There was nothing serious happening in music when I started, not even The Beatles. They were singing 'Love Me Do' and Marvin Gaye... he didn't do 'What's Going On' until the Seventies. (New York, 1985)

Opposite: Tom Petty, Annie Lennox and Dylan.

Now it's just rock, Capital R, no roll, the roll's gone, homosexual rock, working man's rock, stockbroker rock, it's now a highly visible enterprise, big establishment thing. You know things go better with Coke because Aretha Franklin told you so and Maxwell House Coffee must be OK because Ray Charles is singing about it. Everybody's singing about ketchup or headache medicine or something. In the beginning it wasn't anything like that, had nothing to do with pantyhose and perfume and barbecue sauce... you were eligible to get busted for playing it. It's like Lyndon Johnson saying we shall overcome to a nationwide audience, ridiculous... there's an old saying, 'If you want to defeat your enemy, sing his song' and that's pretty much still true. I think it's happened and nobody knows the difference. In the old days, there's a phrase again, you paid the price to play. You could get run out of town or pushed over a cliff. Of course there was always someone there with a net. I'm not trying to paint just one side of the picture. But, you know, it was tough getting heard, it was radical. You felt like you were part of some circus sideshow. Now it's the main event... The best stuff was done without the spotlight before the commentaries and what not... when they come to define it. I think they killed something very important about it. The corporate world, when they figured out what it was and how to use it they snuffed the breath out of it and killed it. What do they care? Anything that's in the way, they run over like a bulldozer, once they understood it they killed it and made it a thing of the past, put up a monument to it and now that's what you're hearing, the headstone, it's a billion dollar business... What I'm telling you is no lie but then again who wants to hear it? You just get yourself worked up over nothing. (New York, 1985)

The Critics

They can't hurt me. Sure they can crush you and kill you. They can lay you out on 42nd and Broadway and put the hoses on you and flush you in the sewer and put you on the subway and carry you out to Coney Island and bury you on the Ferris Wheel. But I refuse to sit here and worry about dying. (New York, 1965)

Stupid and misleading jerks... sometimes these interpreters are - I mean I'm always trying to stay one step ahead of myself and keep changing with the times, right? Like that's a foolish mission. How many roles can I play? Fools, they limit you to their own unimaginative mentality. They never stop to think that somebody has been exposed to experiences that they

With Mick Jagger.

haven't been... anyway it's not even the experience that counts, it's the attitude towards the experience. There is so much misunderstanding by people who are caught up in their own little worlds laid on you... contrary to what some so-called experts believe, I don't constantly 're-invent' myself - I was there from the beginning. I'm also not any seeker or searcher of God knows what, had it all together a while back and can go any kind of way. There's nothing in any of my songs to ever imply that I'm even halfway searching for some lost gold at the end of any great mysterious rainbow - propaganda that's all it is... never have considered myself as an outsider looking in, everything I do is done from the inside out, you know, I'm a mystery only to those who haven't felt the same things I have.
(New York, 1985)

They ask the wrong questions, like, what did you have for breakfast. What's your favourite colour, stuff like that. Newspaper reporters, man, they're just hung-up writers, frustrated novelists, they don't hurt me none by putting fancy labels on me. They got all these preconceived ideas about me, so I just play up to them. (Sheffield, 1965)

Why should you want to know about me. I don't want to know about you. (Newcastle-upon-Tyne, 1965)

If I'd paid attention to what others were saying, the heart inside of me would have died. (Woodstock, 1969)

It's very tiring having other people tell you how much they dig you if you yourself don't dig you. (London, 1966)

How do you decide when to talk to people and when not to?

You think I'm talking now?... I'm surprised you haven't asked these questions like on a Roger Daltrey set, or a Paul McCartney...

I suppose I would if I had been commissioned to.

Well y'know I'm not going to say anything that you're gonna have any revelations about. It's not gonna happen.

So anything you're telling is just like...

No, I'm trying to satisfy your need to probe into my private life and thoughts here and in a way that's not going to embarrass me and hopefully confound me... hopefully not confound me. (Toronto, 1987)

The Fans

There's a thousand, million, billion people out there. There's so many persons outside. I mean, you can't know them all. (Manchester, 1965)

Do you think that a lot of the young people that buy your records understand a single word of what you're saying?

Sure.
You reckon they do?

Sure.

Why do you say they do? How can you be so sure? But they're quite complicated songs aren't they?

Yeah, but they understand them.

How do you know they understand them? Have they told you that they do?

They told me. Haven't you ever heard that song 'She Said So'? (London, 1965)

Would you say that you cared about people particularly?

Well yeah, but we all have our own definitions of all those words.

'Care' and 'people'...

But surely we know what people are?

Do we?
(London, 1965)

*Were you aware of the fact that tonight at the City Hall you had
a greater audience than has been seen there for many years and more
appreciation than has been heard there? The applause was fantastic.
I never heard so much applause and I've been coming here for
quite a while.*

That makes me feel good, y'know. That makes me feel good.
(Sheffield, 1965)

Judas! I don't believe you... you're a liar.
(London, 1966)

*In the hotel I'm staying in I'm in room 801, and in 802 I find there's
a girl called Sara Dylan.*

Really? Jesus!

I had a drink with her and she tells me she's your sister.

Oh boy. What does she look like?

*She says that she looks very like you. She's dark. She's ten years
younger than you are and she has this extraordinary delusion.*

Well, there are people who follow me around and they
have passports and they have drivers' licences and they all
have 'Dylan' as their name, y'know. What can I do about that.
They change their name on their birth certificate and all that.
What are you asking me about it for?

I suppose because I found it slightly frightening.

Why don't you report her to the local constable or something.
She's an impersonator I guess. I don't know.

*One does think about John Lennon getting shot and maybe you
have to worry about something like that... you don't have security people
around you?*

Many times I have security people around me, you just can't see
them that's all. Nobody knows ever who's with me and who's not.
I don't advertise who I'm coming with.

*But is that something that bothers you ever, the idea that because you
are very famous someone who thinks they love you might kill you?*

Well, that's always the case isn't it. I mean aren't you usually
killed by the person that loves you the most, I don't know.
I mean Jesse James was supposedly... some guy got in close to
him who he thought was his close friend. (Toronto, 1986)

t the 30th Anniversary tribute with George
arrison, Roger McGuinn and Tom Petty.

*The other evening at the sort of mock concert you didn't say anything
to the audience. You know, people in the press said that people all turned
up to this thing and Dylan didn't say hello.*

What was I supposed to say hello for? They're nothing to do
with me. I'm there making a movie. Are you serious? Why didn't
you tell them?

*Oh no, I just read it in the paper and that made me wonder why
you didn't just say hello. I would. I'd feel the pressure.*

No matter what you say, it's never enough is it? I could have
gone on and said, 'Hello everybody, how are you doing out
there' and y'know they'd say, 'Play a song Bob, play a song' and
I'd say, 'Oh man, I don't feel like it right now' and that would
be in the press. 'Dylan was there, he was grumpy, he was moody,
he's a recluse, he came out for a few minutes and he went back
into his trailer or something into the seclusion of his own little
kingdom' is what people would say. I'm just actually quoting
you on something that has been said.

So it's always a losing situation?

Not for me because I don't play that game and you
wouldn't either if you were in my shoes. You wouldn't play that
game... Sometimes it's easier to be polite than it is to be rude.
Sometimes the other way around.

How do you judge when?

Instinct.

ringing down the years

The Sixties

I don't think working was on most people's minds - just
to make enough to eat, you know. Most of everybody, anyway,
you had the feeling they'd just been kicked out of something.
It was outside, there was no formula, never was 'main stream'
or 'the thing to do' in any sense. America was still very 'straight',
'post-war' and sort of into a grey-flannel suit thing, McCarthy,
commies, puritanical, very claustrophobic and whatever was
happening of any real value was happening away from that and
sort of hidden from view and it would be years before the media
would be able to recognise it and choke hold it and reduce it
to silliness. (New York, 1985)

A lot of people say the Sixties generation didn't turn
out well - that they didn't live up to their dreams or follow
through or whatever and they may be right. But there still was
a lot that no-one else has been able to do.
(Los Angeles, 1991)

People are always talking about the Sixties and now we
are almost into the Eighties and everybody wants to know
what happened back then. Well in the Sixties, everything that
happened you did because you wanted to. You didn't do it
because you thought you should do it or because it was the thing
to do. Something inside of you told you you wanted to do it.
There was a network all across the country - really. Very small,
but very close, I still see those people travelling around y'know,
they're still hanging in there. But as far as what happened, it will
always be felt just the same way as the Civil War was always felt
into 1870 and 1880. It was just something which was felt by
everyone whether they knew it or not and a lot of people in the
Sixties started all this which is happening now. They just don't
realise it, you know. But the Fifties gave birth to the Sixties too,
don't forget, and in the Fifties it was even rarer... like in the
Sixties it was people caught up on all the be-bop and the
beat movement, or the subterranean culture that was going
on, but it was home-like and it gave you identity.
(Los Angeles, 1979)

The Eighties

You have to get past the keeping-up-with-the times stuff.
It's not about keeping up with the times, being a poet from the
Eighties, rock'n'roller for the Nineties, you don't want to get
trapped... you have to learn all about it all and call it up when
you need it. The old trades are still the most useful, can get you
out of a jam. Everything is crooked now and the signs all point
you the wrong way - it's like we're living at the time of the Tower
of Babel, all our tongues are confused. We're building a tower
to Venus. Where the hell is that? What we are we going to find
there? God? The Bible says, 'Even a fool when he keeps his
mouth shut is counted wise,' but it comes from the Bible, so it
can be cast off as being too, quote, religious. Make something
religious and people don't have to deal with it, they can say it's
irrelevant. 'Repent, the Kingdom of God is at hand.' That scares
the shit out of people. They'd like to avoid that. Tell that to
someone and you become their enemy.

There does come a time, though, when you have to face facts and the truth is true whether you wanna believe it or not, it doesn't need you to make it true... That lie about everybody having their own truth inside of them has done a lot of damage and made people crazy. Did you ever hear that to conquer your enemy, you must repent first, fall down on your knees and beg for mercy? Does West Point teach that? I don't know, I do know that God hates a proud look. It's a messy situation.

People are just parading around in disguises, wearing faces that don't let you know what they think... I'll tell you this much - when you tell somebody your dreams and hopes you better make sure they love you like a brother or your dreams and hopes probably won't come true... You got to be somewhat superstitious to survive. People like to talk about the new image of America but to me it's still the old one - Marlon Brando, James Dean, Marilyn Monroe, it's not computers, cocaine and David Letterman, we gotta get off that - Hedy Lamarr, Dorothy Dandridge, that's my idea of America... and who's improved on it? Some phoney imaginary soldier can kill a hundred thousand people in a foreign country of his own mind but it's a fantasy and it doesn't stick - people, if they had a choice, would still want to be Rhett Butler.

Ron Wood, Dylan and Keith Richards line-up during the dying moments of Live Aid at Philadelphia, 1985.

Maybe in the Nineties or possibly in the next century
people will look upon the Eighties as the age of masturbation,
when it was taken to the limit, that might be all that's going on
right now in a big way... I like to keep my values scripturally
straight though - I like to stay a part of that stuff that don't
change. Actually it's not that difficult - people still love and they
hate, they still marry and have children, still slaves in their minds
to their desires, still slap each other in the face, and say,
'Honey, can you turn off the light' just like in ancient Greece.
What's changed? When did Abraham break his father's idols?
I think it was last Tuesday. God is still the judge and the devil
still rules the world so what's different? No matter how big you
think you are history is gonna roll over you. Sound like a
preacher don't I? To the aspiring songwriter and singer I say
disregard all the current stuff, forget it, you're better off, read
John Keats, Melville, listen to Robert Johnson and Woody
Guthrie. Movies too, I've seen hundreds of them, how many
of them stay with you? *Shane, Red River, On The Waterfront,
Freaks*? Maybe a handful of others... I just saw one the other
night, as soon as it was over, I couldn't remember a thing
about it. Seemed real important at the time though.
(New York, 1985)

People today are still living off the table scraps of the Sixties.
They are still being passed around - the music, the ideas. Look
what's going on today. There used to be a time when the idea of
heroes was important. People grew up sharing those myths and
legends and ideals. Now they grow up sharing McDonalds
and Disneyland. (New York, 1989)

With MGs guitarist Steve Cropper.

From Now Until Then...

What are your plans for the future?

I generally don't even know what I'm doing next week...
I guess my plans are to go on writing, recording and performing
live. My life's been pretty much like this for as long as I can
remember. To tell you the truth, I think that my life is getting
better all the time. I think that the older you are, the better you
get. So I'm gonna keep on for a long time. If you come to see me
when I'm ninety years old, you'll find me on a stage some place.
(Budapest, 1991)

There's no one to my knowledge that isn't surprised by
their longevity, including myself. But it's very dangerous to
plan [far ahead], because you are dealing with your vanity.
Tomorrow is hard enough. It's God who gives you the freedom,
and the days you should be most concerned with are today
and tomorrow. (Los Angeles, 1990)